Gentle Parenting Reimagined

Do you feel like it's a constant battle to get your child or teen to do even the smallest things? Despite all of the parenting advice you've been given, nothing has worked. Maybe you like the idea of Gentle Parenting but how, exactly, can a parent stay gentle in the face of daily disrespect and oppositional behavior?

Gentle Parenting Reimagined offers evidence-based solutions for families stuck at a crossroads. Today's parents are becoming increasingly attentive toward raising loving humans in a peaceful environment that puts their emotional well-being first. This book unlocks proven strategies to help parents connect with their child and have the relationship they desire while vastly reducing—or even eliminating—daily behavioral challenges. Written by a leading child and family expert, this book draws from Dr. Paul Sunseri's 40 years of clinical experience working with oppositional and defiant children and teens. Using real-world examples, the book provides a clear roadmap to help parents manage disrespect, emotion dysregulation (temper tantrums), not listening, problems with homework, being on time for school, and much more. The book provides strategies to preserve the relationship and protect a child's emotional well-being while simultaneously improving their behavior. This book also addresses the unique challenges of the 21st century and considers how to gently parent in the digital age—managing screen time, social media, the technological impacts of the pandemic, and motivating your child to *get things done*. Written in a conversational and accessible style, this book provides parents and caregivers with tools and techniques for reducing conflict, and increasing family connection.

This book is essential reading for parents wanting to create a healthy and happier home environment, as well as for therapists looking to develop their skills in working with challenging children and teens.

Paul Sunseri, Psy.D., is a clinical psychologist and father of four who treats children and adolescents with serious mental health conditions. He is the developer of Intensive Family-Focused Therapy (myIFFT.org), a highly effective form of family-based mental health care.

"Dr. Paul Sunseri's *Gentle Parenting Reimagined* is not just an immensely practical guide, it is also true in recognizing the value of 'relationship first' amidst the challenges facing parents today. Through decades of professional experience, he has a deep understanding of the most challenging behaviors that led him to develop the strategies that have shown to yield results. Finally, a book that understands the parenting experience at the core, reignites hope for change, and promotes deeper connection with our kids and teens."

Mallory Eastman, *LMFT*

"Our family was in a very dark place with our 14-year-old daughter. We tried so many avenues for help, but nothing worked to bring our family together and into the light. The techniques outlined in Dr. Sunseri's book brought sunshine, hopefulness, control, and, most importantly, laughter back into our lives. It's difficult and may even get more challenging for a while, but if you do the work and stay open and consistent with these strategies, positive changes will begin with your child and your relationship with them. I got my beautiful, funny, intelligent, strong, loving daughter back."

Christi S., *Parent*

"Our 12-year-old son was out of control and exhibited pretty much every behavior described in this book. We were at a total loss as to how to help him and life at home was incredibly overwhelming and stressful. Dr. Sunseri taught us each of the interventions outlined in this book, and by finding the right balance between love and accountability, we began to see almost immediate results that were life-changing for us. It was hard work for me to change my approach to our son but that was the key all along. Dr. Sunseri is a master at behavior change and because of these techniques we now can envision a bright future for our son and our family."

Debbie K., *Parent*

Gentle Parenting Reimagined

How to Make It Work with Oppositional and Defiant Kids

PAUL SUNSERI

Routledge
Taylor & Francis Group

NEW YORK AND LONDON

Designed cover image: © Pobytov Getty Images, © Diane Labombarbe
Getty Images

First published 2025
by Routledge
605 Third Avenue, New York, NY 10158

and by Routledge
4 Park Square, Milton Park, Abingdon, Oxon, OX14 4RN

Routledge is an imprint of the Taylor & Francis Group, an informa business

© 2025 Paul Sunseri

Library of Congress Cataloging-in-Publication Data
Names: Sunseri, Paul, author.
Title: Gentle parenting reimagined : how to make it work with
oppositional and defiant kids / Paul Sunseri.
Description: New York, NY : Routledge, 2025. | Includes bibliographical
references and index. | Identifiers: LCCN 2024032591 (print) |
LCCN 2024032592 (ebook) | ISBN 9781032590325 (hardback) |
ISBN 9781032590318 (paperback) | ISBN 9781003452638 (ebook)
Subjects: LCSH: Gentle parenting. | Child rearing. | Parenting.
Classification: LCC HQ769 .S95155 2025 (print) | LCC HQ769 (ebook) |
DDC 649/.1--dc23/eng/20240911
LC record available at https://lccn.loc.gov/2024032591
LC ebook record available at https://lccn.loc.gov/2024032592

ISBN: 978-1-032-59032-5 (hbk)
ISBN: 978-1-032-59031-8 (pbk)
ISBN: 978-1-003-45263-8 (ebk)

DOI: 10.4324/9781003452638

Typeset in Myriad Pro
by KnowledgeWorks Global Ltd.

During my 40-plus years as a psychologist working with strong-willed, oppositional, and defiant kids, I have had the great honor of standing shoulder to shoulder with so many immensely talented colleagues. The work can be so very difficult, but I am in awe of your love and affection for children and their families—it is truly wondrous and inspiring. This book is dedicated to all those who choose to work with challenging kids, and of course, to the equally awe-inspiring parents who raise them..

Contents

Foreword

Young people are struggling more than ever.

This is not hyperbole; statistics support this reality. And unfortunately, what comes with struggling children and teens are parents who feel lost, confused, exhausted, and overwhelmed on how to respond to the behaviors and mental health struggles they are witnessing and experiencing with their child.

As a licensed therapist, Founder and CEO of River Stones Child and Adolescent Treatment, a residential treatment facility specializing in teens, I have witnessed over my 30-year career of treating hundreds of kids and families, especially in the last 15 years, a significant increase in depression, oppositional behavior, anxiety, suicidal thoughts, self-harm, fewer social connections, and family conflict. Parents are desperately in need of guidance and wisdom in how to unlock the mystery of connecting with their child, how to set limits, how to handle technology, how to navigate school problems, and how to have a peaceful home again. What maybe worked with their other kids in the family isn't working with one. It feels like a storm and parents are desperate as to how to navigate through it. If you can relate to this, *you have the right book in your hand!* It was written for you.

If your teen is struggling, you are not alone.

We have seen a marked increase in childhood mental health issues since around 2010–2011. So, what happened around that time that could lead to a decline in mental health? There are many things such as cultural shifts, parents' work schedules, divisive political rhetoric, the effects of media focusing mainly on violence and conflict, and the decline of gratitude, but we can't get away from the effects of the smart phone. It has been well researched and documented that the effects of kids have unfettered access to social media and the internet has been a significant variable in them experiencing higher levels of depression, anxiety, and social problems, all contributing to problems in the family.

The literature shows the more time kids spend on their devices, the more negative effects we see in their behavior, relationships, the way they experience themselves, and the world. Not only are they affected by the content of what they are viewing, they are missing out on key experiences that lead to healthy adolescent development such as free play, conflict resolution, building forts, playing sports, meeting new friends, and even how to handle boredom, an important life skill. Though parents intuitively understand this, they are struggling with how to put the cat back in the bag and find themselves in a quandary: if they take their devices away, the child resents them, blows up, perhaps becomes violent, or threatens every parent's worst nightmare: self-harm. And if they do nothing out of fear or simply because they have no solutions, the damage and frustration continues.

The solution isn't to demonize the smart phone. And certainly, it isn't the only thing that is causing our kids' suffering. The solution is how parents respond to *anything* that threatens our kids' well-being and healthy development in a way that is effective, preserves relationships, minimizes conflict, and brings peace and fun to the family unit.

Certainly, the pandemic wreaked havoc as well on our kid's development at such a crucial time of social growth and integration. Kids were stripped from their social networks, sport teams, church groups, extended family activities, and forced into isolation, often unsupervised, with their primary connection to the world being through social media, social gaming, and the internet. Stress increased with parents and kids alike, which inevitably led to more family conflict and discord. When it was over, many kids found themselves anxious and ill-equipped to return to the real world of relationships and responsibilities. Residential treatment facilities like River Stones, as well as therapists in private practice, were inundated with referrals to treat these challenges. Once again, parents were lost, exhausted, and overwhelmed with how to deal with these never before experienced challenges.

In this book, Dr. Sunseri attacks the most common struggles parents have in parenting the modern child and teen: managing disrespect, yelling, morning routines, social media, technology, homework, and many others, and perhaps most importantly, he provides plan for gentle but firm discipline and limit setting that both preserves relationships and minimizes arguments and chaos. Within these pages, Dr. Sunseri also has interwoven key principles for effectively motivating your child to do the right thing, be respectful, learn responsibility, and to live more harmoniously within the family.

Dr. Sunseri is an intellectual and an academic who has done his work scanning the research, testing, and creating interventions and, most importantly, working in the trenches with families for decades. Many books focus only on parenting principles or philosophical concepts and parents are left wanting practical real-life solutions. This is where Dr. Sunseri shows his genius. He has a particular knack at translating science and experience into hope and *solutions that actually work*.

As an avid reader of anything related to kids and treatment, I haven't seen anything this wise, practical, and succinctly written. It is the best I have seen for parents. It will be required reading for my clinicians and every parent that admits their child to River Stones Child & Adolescent Treatment facility.

Russell Rice, LMFT
Founder/CEO
River Stones Child and Adolescent Treatment

Introduction

The term "gentle parenting" was introduced by psychologist and author Sarah Ockwell-Smith, who described an approach to raising children which emphasizes empathy, respect, and building strong emotional connections with our children. Proponents of gentle parenting maintain that it keeps a focus on building and maintaining the strongest possible relationship with our children, who then, in turn, hopefully grow up to become kind, loving, well-adjusted human beings.

I love this idea. Adopting a calm, nonreactive approach to raising our children, being in tune with them on an emotional level, and navigating the upsets common to family life are all undeniably good things. On this I am in total agreement, and I suspect few would argue against any of that. Here's the truth of it though: calm, gentle parenting is great idea in theory, but in my experience as a child and family psychologist, it can also be really hard to put into practice with more difficult-to-parent kids.

Why? That's because raising an oppositional and defiant child or teen is far from easy. They often push our buttons, sometimes on a daily basis, and even the smallest things can feel like a battle. In a word, oppositional kids and strong-willed kids can be exhausting. Few parents can stay consistently gentle when facing almost constant negative behavior. As someone who has spent the last four decades working with oppositional kids and their families, here's what I've learned: no parent wants to get angry with their children, and no good parent likes it when they do. The problem is kids often behave in ways that can be very frustrating, and frustration can lead to anger.

In my experience, at the beginning of some exchange that has the potential to turn into an argument, parents don't start off by getting mad. *They work their way into it.* I'm not talking about a parent who is just having a garden-variety bad day, one in which we're just unusually stressed or irritable. Sure, sometimes in that case, as a parent, we're just not the best version of ourselves and that happens. I'm talking more about a day when typical life family is unfolding. Most parents are usually pretty reasonable when they ask their kid to do something, or stop doing something, and they generally don't immediately start off in the red zone. But, if the kid doesn't listen, especially when they've been asked to do something *over and over*, then—oh yes—it's game on.

In theory, we all want to be these amazing, gentle parents but, my goodness, putting that into practice is far from easy, especially when raising a strong-willed, argumentative, or highly oppositional kid. I think where the gentle parenting movement falls short is that we all like the idea of being calm, loving parents, but I've found giving that advice alone is going to leave most parents with challenging kids very confused and often feeling as if they've failed somehow. I can't tell you how many parents of harder kids over the years have asked me, "What did I do wrong? Did I make my kid this way?" The answer, at least in most cases, is no. It isn't about making your kid a certain way, it is more about the fact that some kids come into the world just being harder to raise. These kids require a different skill set, and in most cases when parents learn and use the new skills that follow in this book, their children and teens don't seem that hard anymore.

Why do parents who try to follow gentle parenting practices often conclude they're failing at it? It's because you can't get a more difficult-to-parent kid to do their homework, clean their room, or be polite and respectful just by staying calm and gentle. I wish that were true, but in my practice, I've learned that simply isn't the case and telling parents otherwise is a disservice to them.

That being said, I do see staying calm and gentle as a foundational, essential skill when raising a more strong-willed or oppositional kid, which is why I'm talking about it right here at the beginning of this book. You have to buy into this idea and embrace the value of staying calm, gentle, and matter-of-fact (but still firm) in situations that have the potential to become heated or all of the strategies and interventions that I'm going to teach you simply will not work. Parenting with a gentle, loving, attentive, and playful style is the foundation for the new skills that you'll learn in this book.

Think of it like baking a cake. The recipe calls for eggs, flour, milk, and butter, but without all of those ingredients mixed together what comes out of the oven is not going to look anything like a cake.

So, if we don't like getting mad at our kids and generally only start to get upset when we've repeatedly tried everything we can think of to get them to do something (or not do something), it makes sense that in order to stay gentle we've got to know how to change that behavior in the first place. If you could do this more easily, like knowing how to get your child or teen to do more often what you ask and argue less often with you about it, I don't think you'd have much reason to get upset with them at all.

Knowing what to do in the face of frustrating behavior, which is what this book is all about, makes staying gentle a whole lot easier, I promise.

I've been fortunate enough in my practice to have been able to work with really, and I mean *really*, challenging children and teens for a long time. I'm not sure how many in total but it's somewhere in the vicinity of about a thousand kids by now. This book is about everything that I've ever learned about how to help kids be better versions of themselves—how to be kinder, more respectful, less argumentative, and able to make their way through their childhood and teenage years with a whole lot less conflict with the people who love them with all their hearts.

Put simply, this book will help you be a more relaxed, loving, gentle parent by teaching you all of the various, effective behavior-change strategies that I've learned over the years that work great with more challenging children and teenagers.

And, nothing I'm going to teach you here is just something that sounds great on paper or in theory. All of the strategies, interventions, or techniques that follow in this book are ones that I've used myself with many kids over many years.

I think that I have a unique skill set. I started my career working with challenging kids just after I finished my undergraduate degree, and before I went on to earn a Master's degree and eventually a doctorate in psychology. I was very young when I first started, barely over 20 years old, when I was hired to work in a group home for boys with very serious mental health and behavioral challenges. I knew *nothing* about kids, much less kids with behavior problems, and the only reason I got the job was when I was interviewed, I fibbed and said that I did.

I had no idea what to expect from these boys, and to say I was shocked by their behavior would be an understatement. All six of the kids living in the program had tremendous behavior problems. On a daily basis, they would yell, curse at me, spit at me, try to hit or kick me, throws chairs at me, and they would rarely do what I asked them to do. That being said, when they weren't misbehaving, they were also super cute, funny, and a joy to be around.

Nothing in my education even remotely prepared me for the job. In fact, all my classes were completely useless. So, I had to learn as I went along, especially since none of my coworkers knew much about how to help these boys either and we mostly made it up as we went along. Gradually, over time, simply through trial and error (many trials, many errors), I learned what actually works to get a kid to stop cursing at me, telling me no all of the time, hitting me, and everything else that wasn't okay.

These were not interventions and strategies that I learned overnight. It took me years to figure them out. My entire career as a psychologist has been about working with very challenging kids and the parents who are trying their best to raise them. Every technique, strategy, and intervention described in this book has been battle-tested over many years. There is nothing included in this book that I haven't used myself many times with kids, and taught parents to use, so I know they actually work.

Here's another cool thing about my job that makes me qualified to write this book. Not only have I used or taught these interventions over a long period of time, I've also received continuous feedback from kids and their parents as to whether or not they work. I'll implement an intervention or strategy, either myself or ask a parent to, and then in each instance we get to see the result immediately: the kid's behavior changes in a positive direction or it doesn't. The interventions and strategies throughout the book are all derived from a high number repetitions, over and over, and the immediate feedback based on kids' responses have continuously refined the interventions over time.

Here's some rough math that gives you a sense of the number of repetitions over the course of my career. Let's start with my estimate of working with a thousand kids so far. (It might be higher and it might be lower, but that's a pretty good guess.). Now let's calculate the number of interventions and strategies tried with each kid on average. That's a bit harder to estimate. When I worked directly with kids in residential programs, typically I would intervene on each kid's behavior many times per day. However, if I'm just working with parents as I've done more recently, they're doing the actual implementation of the day-to-day interventions, but I still get feedback from the parent as to what worked and what didn't. I think a good rough estimate of the average number of interventions (repetitions) used per kid is between 100 and 300, so let's meet in the middle and call it 200. So, the math is as follows: 1000 kids times 200 interventions per kid is a total of 200,000 repetitions over my 40 years in practice.

That's an awful lot of data to know whether something's going to work with kids in general, as well as the probability of it also working with yours.

I've also learned over time that there exist fundamental truisms about kids, i.e., patterns of behavior and responses to behavioral interventions that hold true for just about all of them. Think of them as like laws of physics, but the kid versions of them. For example, throughout the book we'll talk about pause, earn, and return reinforcement. I can predict with reasonable certainty how a kid is going to respond to it in a given situation simply because that's how all kids (or practically all) respond to it.

Take note here. This book is much more than helping you get your kids to do more of what you want from them, like doing homework, helping around the house, spending less time on devices, being respectful, not arguing with you, and so on, it's also about helping you have the best, closest, and most loving relationship possible with your child or teen. I think of the day-to-day behavioral challenges as barriers that sit between you and your child, which make it harder for you to stay close to them and for them to stay close to you. I want to help you get rid of those barriers so you can finally have the relationship with your child or teen that you'd always hoped for.

It's tough to stay close when everyone is mad or arguing with each other, and when we repeatedly bump up against the same problems every day, over and over again. There exists a natural human tendency that is hardwired into all of us to want connection and be close to our family. However, to do that fully, we need to know what those barriers to closeness are and get them out of the way. That's when gentle becomes a breeze.

Here's something too: I strongly believe that we change other people's behavior by first changing our own. This is a really important concept, one that I see borne out every day in my clinical work with families. So yes, I can help you get your kid to do their homework, be respectful, get off their phones, or whatever, but that all starts with you.

We're going to change your oppositional child or teen's behavior by first changing yours: your kid will respond differently to you because you're responding differently to them. It's that straightforward, I promise.

Here's the truth of it as I've already mentioned: some kids just come into the world harder than others. Temperamental differences, personality traits if you will, that just make some kids a lot more prone to being strong-willed, oppositional, and emotionally reactive. Your kid didn't ask to be this way, they just are. What they need most are parents who can love them fully, calmly, and confidently, but at the same time have high expectations of both their behavior and the kind of human being they ultimately will become.

Here is how this book is laid out. I'm going to begin by talking again about what I think of as the foundational skills, skills that I feel you must acquire before we get into the weeds of behavior change and the various interventions that will do the changing. I highly encourage you to read every chapter of this book in sequence because your knowledge base will build upon itself in layers, and every foundational skill is important in the process. For example, if you struggle with getting your child or teen do their homework, you might be tempted to jump right to that chapter, but I guarantee that won't work. If you try to do that, you'll be reading about concepts and ideas that will be unfamiliar and you won't be able to it pull off. Patience, please!

This would be a good time for a couple of quick disclaimers.

First, as I've said, my practice has always been focused on working with really challenging kids, and what follows in this book are strategies that I know work with both them and with kids whose behavioral problems are less severe. However, if your child or teen is physically aggressive, engages in or threatens to engage in any kind of self-harm, or exhibits other behaviors that are potentially dangerous, you're going to need more than this book. If that's the case, you should find a skilled therapist right away who can help you. Please do not try any of these interventions without professional guidance if the situation in your home is unsafe. If you'd like to learn more, I described the treatment of kids with these more serious challenges in my book, *Family-Focused Treatment for Child and Adolescent Mental Health: A New Paradigm.*

Here's the second disclaimer. In writing this book, I've tried my best to describe the most common behavioral challenges parents face and provide a road map for responding to those challenges in ways that I hope you find helpful. That being said, every kid is unique and every family situation is different. If I neglected to speak to your particular challenge or you're not seeing your own strong-willed child or teen in this book, please accept my apologies in advance.

Okay, now that we have the disclaimers out of the way, let's start our work together.

Before we get into the strategies, techniques, and interventions that reduce conflict, change behavior, and increase peace and connection, let's move to the next chapter and talk about the three most common parenting styles and see which one science tells us is worth paying attention to.

Part I
Foundational Skills

Parenting Styles for a Happy, Healthy, and More Loving Family

1

Researchers have been studying parenting styles for some time, and quite a bit is known about which style tends to produce kids who are most likely to grow up and become reasonably content and psychologically well-functioning adults. I think the science behind this is pretty well established. I'm not including gentle parenting among the three because I don't think it's been around long enough to have been as thoroughly researched. However, I'll tell you which among the three styles gentle parenting mostly closely resembles and describe why it's highly compatible with a gentle approach.

Parenting styles can generally be grouped into three different categories: authoritarian, authoritative, and permissive. Each style is characterized by a distinct approach to raising children, although parents can occasionally have traits from another category. I'm going to start off by talking about the two parenting styles that don't work very well and explain why.

Authoritarian Parenting

Authoritarian parents tend to have a "my way or the highway" orientation toward raising children. They often establish strict rules that kids are expected to follow without question. In fact, an authoritarian parent would consider being questioned by their child or teen highly disrespectful and would likely provoke some sort of a disciplinary response. There is very little emphasis placed on open communication or flexibility, and little room for any sort of compromise or negotiation. Typically, there is an overreliance on the use of punishment, which tends to be overly strict and often more excessive than is necessary to correct unwanted behavior.

DOI: 10.4324/9781003452638-2

Authoritarian parenting was more common in the past than it is currently. Its use was probably most common of what's referred to as the "Silent Generation," the generation born between the years 1925 and 1945. The term Silent Generation first appeared in a *Time* magazine article in 1951, and it was so named because those born during that time period experienced both the Great Depression and World War II. They were expected not to complain, keep their heads down, and they typically adhered to traditional values, had respect for others, and had a strong work ethic. This is the generation that parented the Baby Boomers, those born between the years 1946 and 1964.

I was raised with an authoritarian style, or at least partially, so I can speak to what it's like having lived through it. My stepfather was highly authoritarian, and my mother unfortunately left most of the disciplining up to him. I'm not sure if Child Protective Services was around back then, but if so, they should have been a frequent visitor to our house. None of it seemed really all that unusual to me because most of my friends were parented that way too. Probably the only good that came out of experiencing an authoritarian style was that I remember very clearly making a conscious decision as a young man that I would never parent my own kids that way. I think this is probably true of many of my generation, and while some of this style still leaked into our own parenting, we were far less authoritarian than our own parents.

Unfortunately, the authoritarian style is still alive and well. I don't see it as often in my practice as I used to, but trust me, there are still plenty of authoritarian parents out there.

One of the concerns of authoritarian parenting is that kids raised in that environment often struggle as teenagers and adults. An authoritarian style is very effective for getting kids to be compliant, or at least appear that way, but it comes with an enormous price tag. Research has shown that children with authoritarian parents tend to have anger issues, are more aggressive, have lower self-esteem, and are more rebellious in later adolescence and adulthood. In addition, I find that kids raised with an authoritarian style tend not to have very close relationships with their parents, are resentful of them, and leave home as soon as they can. Think of it this way: most military recruits in basic training aren't particularly close to their drill sergeants—human beings just don't work that way.

Kids with authoritarian parents, while they can appear outwardly well behaved, still break plenty of rules, but they just get really good at making sure they're not caught.

Permissive Parenting

Permissive parents tend to be warm and nurturing, but they often have minimal or no expectations of their kids in terms of their behavior and hence aren't great at limit setting. In my experience, they act more like friends to their kids rather than parents. It's always trouble when I hear a parent say, "My daughter and I are best friends." Kids don't need their parents to be their friends; they need them to be their parents. That includes having rules, boundaries, and expectations for their behavior and how they treat others. We'll talk more in just a bit about the importance of setting limits with strong-willed and oppositional kids, and getting really good at that as a parent is vital for you to have a peaceful family life.

The research on children with permissive parents shows that they are often aimless, domineering, entitled, low achievers, and far more prone to emotional upsets. In truth, for people outside the immediate family, these kids are sometimes hard to be around because they tend to run the show and can make others miserable.

I suspect the advent of permissive parenting and the recent move toward its close cousin, helicopter parenting, has occurred as a backlash to the authoritarian style of earlier generations. However, like any pendulum that swings, it can often go much too far in the wrong direction.

Helicopter parents tend to be highly involved in their kids' lives and overly protective of them. These parents are excessively focused on safety, often to the point where kids are not given developmentally normal opportunities to become more independent and self-sufficient. In my book, *Treating Child and Adolescent Mental Health: A New Paradigm*, I wrote extensively about the link between helicopter parenting and the increase in depression, anxiety, and suicide among children and teens. As a society, we've moved away from allowing kids to have unsupervised time away from their parents to practice skills that lead to self-reliance and independent decision-making. Instead, by adopting an overly protective style, we are teaching children to be fearful and become overly dependent on their parents rather than learning how to make decisions for themselves.

So, authoritarian parents are too rigid and controlling, and permissive parents don't set limits when they should. Neither style results in particularly good outcomes for kids. If only there was a parenting style that was somewhere in the middle, the Goldilocks of parenting styles. Let's see what that is.

Authoritative Parenting

This third style of parenting finds a middle path between an authoritarian and a permissive style, allowing for the best of both worlds. Not surprisingly, children of authoritative parents tend to have the best life outcomes. They are more likely to be confident, responsible, thoughtful of others, and have higher self-esteem. They also tend to be friendly, self-reliant, self-controlled, cooperative, more oriented to achievement, and have better mental health.

In addition, authoritative parents tend to have a close, supportive relationship with their children. They foster a sense of independence and self-reliance, giving kids opportunities to make their own decisions when possible, but not to a degree that is beyond their developmental level. Authoritative parents step in when they need to, but often hang back to let their kids explore the world and make their choices, even in situations in which they might fail. They are also far more likely to negotiate things with their kids in a flexible, easy way, but they are also firm and not negotiating everything.

For example, let's say a 4th grader wanted to wear something really unusual to school. They've picked out some kind of clothing choice that's a bit unusual and might cause them to be teased at school. An authoritarian parent would just forbid the kid from wearing the outfit without any further discussion. A permissive parent wouldn't pay much attention at all to what the kid was wearing or would just let them to wear whatever they wanted and see it as a form of healthy self-expression.

An authoritative parent would land somewhere in the middle. They would definitely conclude that it's probably not the best idea for the child to wear that outfit to school, but they wouldn't just outright forbid it. An authoritative parent would talk to their child about it, likely something to the kid along the lines of gentle advice giving. They'd hope their advice would influence the kid in a positive direction such that they picked out something else to wear. ("Hmm. I haven't seen you wear that before. Not sure if those colors go together. I'm wondering if this might look better on you?") If the child still wanted to wear the outfit, the parent would be easy about it and let them, hoping that the feedback from other kids at school would be enough to affect their clothing choice the next day.

If their kid reported back that no one commented on their outfit or seemed to care much about it, an authoritative parent would probably just let it go and decide what the kid wears isn't a big deal (a "hill not worth dying on"). A clothing thing is also what I refer to as a self-correcting problem, i.e., one where as a parent you probably don't have to do anything about it at all because in a few months the kid will probably dress differently anyway. However, if some teasing at school did occur, an authoritative parent wouldn't have any problem stepping in at that point and setting some sort of reasonable limit to protect the child from more teasing ("Look I know you love it, but you have to wear another outfit. You were teased yesterday and I don't want that to happen again today. Change into something else please.").

Authoritative parents are very loving, communicative, and warm, but they also have very high expectations of their child or teen, and they set limits in a fair, firm, consistent, and matter-of-fact way. The gentle parenting movement is all about the first part; it does that part really well, but with less emphasis on the second part.

Why Limit Setting Is Essential for Kids but Especially for Strong-Willed and Oppositional Kids

One of the important lessons that I've learned working with challenging kids and their families, along with raising four of my own, is that all kids need limits.

Not just need them; they actually want them. I've learned that kids do not like behaving in negative ways—not following rules, being disrespectful to their parents, not helping out around the house, not doing their homework, and so on. They don't feel good about themselves when they do those things, and they know it's wrong. From the time they are born, kids just *behave*—they try out all kinds of new behavior not knowing what's okay and what isn't. They mean no harm and are just doing what kids do: exploring life and trying to understand where the guardrails are. Kids need feedback from their parents on what's okay and what isn't in order to turn into the human beings we hope them to become.

All kids push limits, although obviously some harder than others. When they push, what is most comforting and reassuring to them is encountering a solid object. By solid object, I mean limits on their behavior set by you as their parent ("That isn't okay with me"). Again, not in a harsh or authoritarian way, but in a way that blends kindness while still being firm. When kids push (misbehave) and then encounter a clear but loving limit, they seem to relax, taking comfort knowing where the limit is and that someone will stop them from stepping over it again.

However, when kids don't encounter that solid object (no limit), or when the object is there sometimes and not others (an inconsistent limit), they tend to push even harder. It's sort of like they're trying to see how far they can go, waiting for someone to finally say enough. I find that kids are far more anxious in a family system in which there are either no limits or inconsistent limits. They know what they're doing is wrong, feel bad about doing it, and are wondering when someone will finally just tell them no and actually mean it. Oppositional and defiant kids and teenagers especially need fair and firm limits placed on their behavior because in comparison with easier-to-parent kids, they push harder for limits far more often.

I think that due to the pendulum shift that I mentioned earlier, many of the parents I see in my practice have shied away from setting limits. Well, let me qualify that. They're good at setting limits, saying something like "You need to complete your missing homework assignments." That's definitely a limit, i.e., that it's not okay to have missing assignments. However, it's the follow-through on enforcing the limit (making sure it's followed) that often gives parents trouble. Many parents tell their kids over and over again to do something, or not do something, which is the first half of limit setting (having an expectation), but it does not include the second half: taking the steps necessary to make sure the expectation has been met.

I feel gentle parenting in many cases is very hard to pull off because while kids need their parents to listen to them, be understanding and empathic, kids just as much need to be told no.

Following through on a no with difficult-to-parent kid is a lot harder. However, once they encounter that solid object from an authoritative and gentle parent, they generally respond to it and become happier, healthier, and better versions of themselves. Throughout this book, I'm going to teach you how to enforce limits peacefully but effectively.

Giving Off the Right Demeanor or "Vibe"

This idea can be a hard one for parents, but I've found it's really important for raising strong-willed and oppositional kids. It's about your presentation (your demeanor) when asking a kid to do or not do something, or when they are acting out and the situation calls for some kind of limit setting. How you come across in these moments can make a big difference in terms of how your child or teen is going to respond to you and accept the limit.

I've found that what works best is to adopt a calm, matter of fact, and confident vibe. This can be hard at first, especially if the negative behavior in question is off-putting. I learned this years ago when I worked in residential treatment programs. I had the privilege of having several coworkers who were able to pull this off beautifully no matter what the kid was doing. These coworkers were unflappable. A kid might be cursing at them, screaming at them, saying something threatening, very often all at the same time. It would be easy to react to this kind of behavior, maybe get angry or feel intimated, and show that in facial expressions or body language, but they never did. They looked very at ease and confident, and no matter what the kid said or did, they didn't outwardly react to it. These amazing people also rarely engaged the angry kid in a back-and-forth conversation or tried to reason with them (we'll talk about the rationale for this in Chapter 2), and they came across as relaxed and super confident. However, I don't think the confidence was just an act. They were confident because they knew exactly what to do and say in response to the behavior and were certain they could eventually get the kid to calm down and resolve the situation peacefully. (Everyone calms down eventually.)

This is the demeanor that I teach parents when they are setting limits with their kids because it works so well. I think it's comforting for a kid who's emotionally dysregulated or out of control to see an adult who isn't freaking out in response. It's sort of like saying "Hey, I've got you," and I think kids find safety and reassurance in that. It's not being a robot; it's about not being reactive, angry, or intimidated.

If you're looking for a really good example of an authoritative parent with a great demeanor, watch or rewatch the movie *To Kill a Mockingbird*. The character of Atticus Finch is very much an authoritative parent to his two young children who regularly get into trouble. He's warm, kind, and attuned to his kids, but he also gives off a very relaxed, confident vibe and has no trouble setting limits.

Changing your demeanor might be hard for you at first, especially before you've learned the strategies and skills contained throughout this book. It's hard not looking anxious or intimidated when that's exactly how you're probably feeling. I tell parents that giving off a confident and relaxed vibe is like being an actor—no matter what you're feeling on the inside, it's important not to show that on the outside. True confidence will come later once you've learned and practiced exactly how to respond to whatever behavior your child sends your way.

Chief takeaways from Chapter 1

- Science has told us a lot about parenting styles and which one most often results in the happiest and healthiest kids.
- An authoritarian style is often too punitive and inflexible (the opposite of gentle parenting), and a permissive style doesn't provide kids with enough clear rules or expectations. Kids raised in either environment can have problems, especially in later life.
- An authoritative style is in the middle—kind, loving parents who are flexible but still have high expectations of their kids' behavior while also setting fair and firm limits.
- Kids with authoritative parents tend to be more confident, friendly, responsible, self-reliant, self-controlled, more achievement oriented, and have better mental health. This style is highly compatible with gentle parenting.
- All kids need fair and firm limit setting, especially oppositional children and teenagers. In the absence of that, they'll often keep pushing limits more and more, all the while knowing it's wrong and not liking themselves for doing it (and wanting you to stop them).
- Kids who are strong-willed can often make their parents feel angry, scared, or intimidated. A relaxed, confident, matter-of-fact demeanor in the face of off-putting behavior is highly effective, even if it means pretending to be confident well before you actually are.

How to Become a
No Yelling Family

2

Here's the thing that every parent secretly knows and will often say out loud to me: yelling works. It's true.

By "works," I mean when we raise our voice at our kids, they will often finally do what they're asked. I'm not sure if that's because we scare them into doing it or they think we are finally serious, or maybe both. I'm not saying that parents feel good about yelling, but it really does get the job done sometimes. The problem is yelling comes with an enormous, albeit invisible, price tag.

Typically, it goes like this: a parent will ask a kid nicely (or at least neutrally) to do something, like empty the dishwasher, pick up their room, stop hiding out in their bedroom, do their homework, put down their phone, or whatever. Most kids don't just flat-out say "No, I'm not going to do it." (Most anyway, but we'll talk more about the ones who do and how to make that work too.) Usually, you'll get a half-hearted "okay" from them, but as every parent reading this book already knows, this in no way means they're actually going to do it, far from it.

That puts you in a position of having to nag, asking your kid over and over again to do something, which ultimately is annoying to them and you. Kids will tell us to stop nagging them (who wants to be nagged after all?), which is an ironic thing for them to say because their own behavior (not doing what's been asked) puts you in a position of doing the nagging in the first place. Of course, if they'd just done what you told them to do, then you'd have no reason to nag. However, if you've ever tried to make this argument with a kid, you know that goes exactly nowhere.

So, we ask nicely a few times. Then, we become progressively irritated because they still haven't done it, and then we're *really* irritated to the point where we yell "I'M NOT TELLING YOU AGAIN. DO IT RIGHT NOW!" Remember, as I said earlier, we don't start off mad, but rather work our way into it. And guess what, they often finally listen. You're not happy

DOI: 10.4324/9781003452638-3

though because you had to yell at them, and they're certainly not happy about being yelled at.

Let's deconstruct all this from a psychologist's perspective. To do so, I first need to introduce a term we'll be using often in this book: *reinforcement*. Put in really simple terms, a behavior is *positively reinforced* if something occurs immediately after the behavior that we like, want, or make us feel good, which in turn then makes it more likely that we'll behave that way again. I'm sure you've heard of the term positive reinforcement before, and there are countless real-world examples of it:

- Letting a kid stay up past bedtime because they had a really good day.
- Getting an "A" on a well-written essay.
- A cheering audience after a team scores a goal.
- Making a meal that everyone tells you they love.
- Every paycheck you've ever received, and so on.

Most of the books and podcasts on gentle parenting tell you that positive reinforcement works the best and we should try to only use that with our kids, and I agree to a point. There is substantial research that shows positive reinforcement is an effective way to change behavior, and I recommend that you use it as often as you can. However, I've learned that with strong-willed and oppositional children and teens, positive reinforcement alone is not going to work all that well. Most kids are going to need some sort of blend between positive reinforcement and reasonable consequences, but we'll talk more about this in subsequent chapters.

Here's a bit of a prelude to what follows in the book. There's also something called *negative reinforcement,* a terrible name for something because the name alone does a really bad job of telling you what it actually is. It's also a concept that I've found to be very confusing to most people. Negative reinforcement is weird and hard to understand, so much so that I'd be willing to bet that if you lined up a bunch of therapists and asked them what negative reinforcement is, there's a pretty good chance most would think it means punishment which is something different altogether. I'm going to be talking a whole lot more about negative reinforcement later in this book (what I've renamed pause, earn, and return reinforcement), and once you understand how to use it with your kids, it's going to become your new best friend. (And, if you're wondering, no, despite its name it's not the slightest bit negative or punitive. But, my goodness, it's a powerhouse.) For now, here's a simple way to understand negative reinforcement: it's when a person has to behave in a certain way in order to stop something undesirable from occurring. When that person's behavior brings an end to something undesirable, their behavior has been negatively reinforced (told you it was confusing). Think of it this way: you have to do something to stop something that you don't like. Some real-world examples include

- Opening your umbrella to keep you dry. (Opening the umbrella is the behavior that keeps you from getting wet. Opening the umbrella has been negatively reinforced.)
- Opening a window to get your smoke alarm to stop making a racket.
- Eating a sandwich when you're hungry.
- Turning on the air conditioner when you get hot.
- Paying an overdue bill to get a utility turned back on.
- A teenager losing their phone until they've been respectful again for a while.
- Not allowing a kid to spend time with friends on the weekend until they finish all their homework.

If you're not getting the idea of negative reinforcement yet, don't worry because, like I said, we'll come back to it later.

Okay, now that you know what positive reinforcement is, and maybe have a rough idea of what negative reinforcement is, let's go back to our yelling scenario.

Here's the thing: when parents yell and then a kid complies, *everyone is reinforcing everyone else but in the completely wrong way.*

To start, the parents have learned that asking something calmly doesn't work, meaning the kid didn't do what was asked of them when they were nice about it. So much for gentle. But, when you finally raise your voice, although you don't feel particularly good about it, and your child or teen then finally complies, that teaches you that yelling works. Your yelling was reinforced because the kid finally did what was asked, making it far more likely that you're going to yell again. That's thing about reinforcement—you don't need to know that you've been reinforced for it to change your behavior. Most reinforcement, in fact, takes place well outside of our conscious awareness.

Here's what we also know about reinforcement: what gets reinforced, gets repeated.

The reinforcement that occurs on your kid's side of the equation is as follows. First, they have clearly learned to ignore your request when made nicely. There are a lot of good reasons for this. First, I'm sure there have been situations in which you've asked your child or teenager a few times to do something but then you just got busy and forgot all about it. The kid has learned (and been reinforced for) adopting an avoidance (a do-nothing) strategy. ("Lots of times my parents ask me to do something and then they just forget about it.") I suspect this works just often enough for the behavior to become set in place (intermittently reinforced for the psychologists reading this book).

Second, in my experience, parents often give up asking out of frustration and just do the thing themselves. ("I don't like all the fighting so it's easier for me to just do it.") In this situation, the kid learns if they hold out long enough, they'll might never have to do it. Resistance, therefore, is definitely not futile. By giving up and doing the task yourself, your kid's resistance has been massively reinforced. It's also the case that some kids just refuse to do something and you simply don't know how to get them to do it, so being oppositional gets reinforced every time the kid is let off the hook.

Finally, there is an element of negative reinforcement coming into play here too because when the kid finally does what's been asked, the parents stop nagging and yelling at them.

Again, there's not much gentle anywhere to be found here. Who can stay calm and matter-of-fact during all of this? Please understand too that there's no judgment on my part for any family in this situation. No one knows, neither the parent nor the kid, that their behavior is the natural product of reinforcement. As parents, understandably, we just want something done when we ask our kids to do it, and kids, understandably, sometimes don't want to do things (which is true of us adults too, right?). No bad kids, no bad parents, you're just a family with good intentions who love each other getting caught up in a pattern of behavior that you've inadvertently learned and taught each other despite realizing you've done so.

A quick word on spanking here. I've so far been talking about yelling, but spanking is an even bigger response to a kid breaking a rule or not listening. The same principles of reinforcement apply here too, i.e., if spanking changes behavior, you're going to be more likely to spank again. Thankfully, spanking has become less common over the years, but I vote that it disappears completely. It's such an odd idea way of looking at things in my opinion. When an adult strikes another adult, that's a crime and brings with it serious penalties, as well as it should. But, somehow, kids are exempt—you can physically strike this smaller, weaker person and somehow that's okay? At the same time, we also teach our kids not to get physical with other kids and talk out their problems, but then we solve family problems ourselves with force? It makes no sense to me. Every so often I'll work with a parent who's reluctant to stop spanking and here's what I say to them: "If I could show you how to raise kids who are respectful and do what you ask them to do without every laying a hand on them, would you be interested?" Thankfully, everybody says yes to this and it's 100% true. Spanking needs to stop.

To change the getting-angry-at-your-kids scenario, we're going to need to replace this unhelpful reinforcement pattern with a different one that works far better. That was a bit of a tease on my part because I'm not going to tell you how to do that just yet as we're not quite done with the rationale for gentle parenting. As I said, being gentle (calm, matter-of-fact, and loving) is a foundational skill, and I really want you to buy into the idea before I teach you the stuff that works to get oppositional and defiant kids to follow your directions.

Later in the book I'm going to teach you how to get your kids to do what's asked of them the first time you ask them (okay, you might need to ask them twice on occasion, but not more than that, I promise). They'll do it because once you get out of the habit of nagging or yelling at them, they'll start to listen to your calm and reasonable voice, not the angry one. And they'll do what's asked of them because we're going to give your kids incentives (good reasons) for doing so. All human beings respond to incentives; we're all far more likely to do something if there's something in it for us. That's just the truth of it. And by incentives, I don't mean bribes, monetary or otherwise, we're just going to give your kids good reasons for doing what's asked. These will be fair, reasonable, and above all, kind. I'm a great believer in teaching parents what works, but every strategy and intervention I teach you is also going to be gentle. You'll be reinforced for using these strategies in a calm, peaceful way because they'll work for you, and your kids will be reinforced because they'll get what they want out of it too, all without anyone ever needing to raise their voice.

Making the Commitment to Become a No-Yelling Family

"Really, you're going to ask me to never raise my voice at my child or teenager?" Yes, that's exactly what I'm going to ask, and I wouldn't ask it of you if I didn't think you could do it. This is 100% doable, not just by a psychologist, but it's also within reach of every parent who practices and then acquires the right set of skills. I can say this with some confidence because I work every day with parents who learn how to pull it off.

Am I asking for perfection and for you to never raise your voice with your kids? No, I'm definitely not asking for that because it doesn't seem realistic. However, I am asking that you get yelling down as close to zero as you possibly can.

I'm the father of four adult daughters and I'm happy to say that I don't ever recall raising my voice with them. I'm not telling you this to say that I'm all that, only to let you know it can be done. I'm certain though that had I not had years of practice learning how to do this with other people's kids, I probably would not have gotten it right with my own. It just takes a strong commitment to not raising your voice and practicing it enough to get the hang of it.

Let me give you other really good reasons as to why you'd want to strongly commit to becoming a no-yelling family. By the way, this goes both directions—I'm hoping that you rarely or never yell at your kids, and at the same time, we'll get them to be less likely to yell at you too (and if they do, you'll know exactly how to change that).

First, isn't this really what you want to model for your kids? That people who care about each other communicate and solve problems together in a peaceful, respectful, and loving way? The reality is, though, that we sometimes, or even often, model the opposite in our family. In truth, I think we save our worst behavior for the people we love the most. We lose our temper with them, sometimes speak to them harshly, and say unkind things in the heat of the moment that we would never say to anyone else in almost any other context or situation. When your boss pulls you into their office because they're unhappy with you, justifiably so or not, you're very likely not going to scream at them. Instead, you'll try and stay calm, and do your best to choose your words carefully so as not to say anything that makes it worse.

Can we honestly say that we put that same amount of effort into how we treat others at home? I don't think so, not most of us anyway. I believe we have all of this backward. It's our family who, above all others, deserves to be treated in the kindest, most loving way. I think we make a choice in terms of in what contexts or situations it's acceptable to raise our voice, and in what contexts it isn't, and then we follow that rule to the detriment of our relationships with our loved ones.

I'm trying to encourage you to establish that same culture and value within your own family—*no one gets to raise their voice and speak in an unkind way*. We certainly hope our children communicate with us in a kind, gentle way. By parents modeling for them that we can get through challenges and tough situations and still be gentle with each other, our kids will extend that same value (and behavior) into all of their other relationships too, with friends, siblings, and someday their future spouses or partners. I've learned that kids watch and absorb what we do, not what we say we do, and they are very keen observers.

As I mentioned in the introduction, when I was younger working in residential treatment programs with children and teenagers, I would routinely be on the receiving end of negative, and sometimes even scary, behavior. I quickly learned, however, that I could *never* raise my voice with these kids because the effect of doing so was immediate and obvious: whatever behavior I was dealing with before got much worse. Mine is not the only profession that has figured this out. Good classroom teachers don't raise their voices with students either, nor do nurses and doctors with unruly patients. They are firm and unflappable. Yelling at students or patients is not just unprofessional, it correctly makes angry people even angrier.

Here's something else to consider. Not only does it make everyone in the family feel bad when we raise our voices, but kids absolutely stop listening to you in any meaningful way and judge you heavily for doing so.

I want to tell you a story that one of my patients told me, which illustrates this point. I worked with a father who came to therapy because he had a temper with his kids and he wanted to work on it (which I greatly admired him for doing). He had made the decision that he didn't want to be that kind of dad, the one that blows up at his kids (a boy and a girl). One day he was driving them to school, and at the time, they would have been in their early teens, around age 13 or 14. Both kids were together in the backseat and the boy, as kids sometimes do, had a tendency to pick on and tease his younger sister. He started in on her and she said to her father, "Dad, Daniel is teasing me." The dad, quite reasonably said, "Daniel, cut it out." The boy stopped. A few minutes later, though, he started back up and the dad again said, "Daniel I said cut it out" and the boy again stopped.

By this time, the girl had had enough of her brother and just tried to ignore him, so she turned away and started texting a friend. A few minutes later, Daniel was right back at it and the girl said, "Dad, make him stop!" Now the dad was fed up, and at the top of his lungs yelled, *"Goddammit, Daniel, I told you to STOP!"* This time Daniel stopped once and for all because at this point, he knew his dad was serious.

The two kids were dropped off at school and the dad didn't think much about this again until a few days later when just by chance he looked through his daughter's text messages. He found the exchange she had with her friend in the car while all of this was happening. It said: *"My dad's being an ass and he's yelling at my brother."* Whoa. Not that her brother was being an ass for teasing her, and let's be honest the kid kind of was being an ass, but my dad's being an ass even though he came to her aid.

So sure, when we yell at our kids, they'll finally listen, but they won't respect us, and any information of value that we're trying to impart to them will be immediately dismissed and ignored. Plus, as this story teaches us, they'll see you as the bad guy on top of everything else even if you're trying to help.

At its core, this book is not about just getting strong-willed and oppositional kids to do things the way we want them to. That's obviously a part of it, true. But that's not the real prize, is it?

The Idea of "Relationship First"

I absolutely want there to be less conflict and upset in your family. I also want you to be able to successfully navigate any challenges and issues that arise, to know how to deal with any sort of behavior issue that might become a potential source of conflict, and have most days be as peaceful and loving as possible.

However, what I really want, and I think you do too, is for you to have a great, loving relationship with your child and for them to have that with you. I want them to be able to open up to you, to feel safe coming to you, including about topics that are hard or embarrassing, and to seek you out as a source of love, comfort, and support at those times in which they need it the most. Not just now, when they're kids, but for the rest of their lives, and yours.

This book is really about relationships.

There's a concept, an idea, that I call "relationship first." Put simply, it means that in any interaction with your child, small or large, any topic of conversation, any problem that needs solving, any behavior that needs changing, it's the relationship between you and them that counts the most. That's the prize, and if you keep your relationship as your highest priority, your overarching goal, that is what will ultimately guide us through every aspect of parenting, both now and forever.

In truth, people often don't do that—they get stuck on things that don't matter. Winning an argument, proving a point. The thing of the moment becomes the priority, not the relationship itself. Relationship first isn't about winning the argument, it's about being mindful in every interaction, and in dealing with any problem that needs solving, to choose a course of action that preserves your relationship with your child, or even, ideally, enhances it. Some examples of this might be

- How can I get my kid to do their homework with the least amount of conflict and upset, while making my relationship with them even better at the same time?
- What if my kid develops views on a topic that run counter to my own (for example, political or religious views, gender identity, sexual preference, and so on)? How can I navigate those differences peacefully, and respectfully, while at the same time remaining close and still being a source of influence to them in a helpful way?
- What if something REALLY bad happens, something I thought my kid would never do—how am I going to respond and solve the problem (stay effective) while not doing anything along the way that causes harm to our relationship?
- What if I want them to be straight-A students, but school is hard for them? How do we navigate those years and still be close?

If my relationship with my child comes first, if that's what really matters to me, then I'm going to use that priority to guide every decision I make along the way, while at the same time remaining true to my values of being gentle, loving, and kind. Committing to gentle parenting and not raising your voice is the first step in making that happen, along with other skills that we'll be talking about in the next chapters.

Let's turn our attention in the next chapter to patterns of communication that don't work with our kids and replace them with ones that do.

Chief takeaways from Chapter 2

- Reinforcement, both positive and negative, are really important concepts when it comes to understanding and changing family dynamics.
- Many times, usually without our awareness, we actually reinforce (make stronger) each other's behavior in the wrong ways. Kids not doing what they're asked, and parents sometimes raising their voices in response, is an example of that which can be changed for the better—no yelling, and getting things done without nagging or upsets.
- What gets reinforced, gets repeated.
- We often save our worst behavior for the people who we love the most. It's true. We wouldn't dream of raising our voices or speaking harshly to other important people in our lives, like our boss, for example. For some reason, these rules are often suspended at home.
- Changing this starts with making a strong commitment as a family to do otherwise and learning the strategies and techniques in this book to make that much easier.
- "Relationship first" is a concept, which can serve as a guide for all of our important relationships. When we put our relationships with our kids first (our highest, most important priority), every interaction we have with them, or any situation we try to navigate, should preserve our relationship with them, or ideally even enhance it while still solving the problem at hand.
- Please consider becoming a no-yelling family. I promise it's doable even with very challenging kids, and you'll be so happy you did.

Part II

Improving Communication

The Expectation of Having Expectations

3

In the previous two chapters, we have covered some of the foundational skills that I believe are essential to being able to best parent an oppositional child or teen. You really have to start with these and get good at them, so much so that I never teach parents the behavior change strategies covered in the later parts of this until I'm sure the essential foundational skills are in place.

These skills include

- Gentle parenting but with an authoritative style.
- Making the commitment to becoming a no-yelling family, and staying calm and matter-of-fact no matter what negative behavior your child is throwing in your direction.
- Embracing the principle of relationship first.

Let us now turn our attention to the idea of effective limit setting and how to set good limits within the context of a gentle style. As I've mentioned before, the gentle parenting movement places a really great emphasis on how to be good to your kids but it's almost completely silent as to what to do when they're not being good to you.

I also mentioned that all kids want and need limits. Setting limits is an important part of parenting. However, I think the gentle parenting movement has moved the needle too far in the permissive direction and too far away from holding kids accountable when they do something that isn't okay. As I mentioned previously, there are two essential ingredients in setting limits with kids: making your expectations known, and then, when necessary, holding them accountable for those expectations. I find that most parents are pretty good at the first but not so great at the second, especially at this particular moment in our culture.

DOI: 10.4324/9781003452638-5

I strongly encourage you to have high expectations of your kids. The expectation that they treat you and others respectfully and kindly, that they don't do or say things to you or anyone else that might be hurtful, to be responsible and take responsibility, and to be honorable, resilient, independent, capable, hardworking, and thoughtful. Set a high bar for them and express confidence in their ability to meet these expectations. By creating this expectation early with children, and all throughout their young lives, coupled with your love, guidance, and support, this will bring out the very best in them.

However, I regularly encounter parents who set the bar of expectations far too low. Not because they don't want their kids to be their best, but slowly, over time, some parents come to believe that their strong-willed and oppositional child or teen can't meet those high expectations and so the expectations become watered down. For example, many of the kids I work with regularly curse at their parents. Of course, cursing doesn't start overnight, but when their kids start to slip into this mode, it's hard for parents to stop it. Over time, the cursing becomes a habit and the new norm in the family. No parent likes being cursed at, but parents often see that as an inevitability of the kid's oppositional nature or their mental health condition.

I've had countless parents tell me their child or teen loses their temper because they have ADHD or some other disorder. This becomes part of the family story, and once the kid then buys into that story, they'll often use it often to justify their behavior. They might say they can't do their homework because they have ADHD, depression, or anxiety. I'm not saying that ADHD or what have you might not make doing homework more difficult, but if a parent starts to agree with this argument, the bar of expectations has now been dropped significantly and in a very unhelpful way.

When the bar of expectations is low, kids will hit that low bar and go no higher. However, when you raise the bar, it might take some time and be a bumpy ride for a while, but many kids ultimately rise to the expectation and will do far better than you (or they) might have thought possible.

The childhood mental health epidemic is currently a serious problem. Articles about it are in everyone's newsfeed, it's all over social media, talked about in schools, and so on. Much of that is a good thing in that mental illness is now less stigmatized, mental health resources are far more accessible, and psychological treatments get better every day. There is a downside to this, however. It's now easier than ever to get a diagnosis for something, and kids are much more likely than ever before to get labelled with a mental health condition. A diagnosis, while valid in many instances, also makes it very easy to lower the bar of expectations of kids ("I can't do this because I have this or that").

In my book, *Treating Child and Adolescent Mental Health: A New Paradigm*, I spoke extensively about this watering down of expectations for children and adolescents with serious mental health conditions. I made the argument, hopefully convincingly, that the over-diagnosing of kids hasn't been helpful, and a vital component of effective treatment for kids with depression, anxiety, and self-harm includes "righting the ship." i.e., not watering down expectations but instead keeping expectations high.

As I said, I'm in total agreement that kids with a mental health condition are going to find it harder to do certain things, *but they need to do those things any*way. There are a lot of kids with ADHD who still do their homework, or kids with depression and anxiety who still make it to school. In fact, the treatment for school avoidance includes helping kids go to school despite them not wanting to (avoidance). Put simply, the treatment for depression isn't spending more time in a darkened bedroom.

As James Lehman said, when you excuse a kid from the normal responsibilities of life, you're treating them as if they are damaged goods. This is not the message we should be sending to our kids.

It is a normal and healthy expectation that kids not curse at their parents, that they are respectful, kind, responsible, take responsibility, work hard, and so on. Raise the bar and you'll be amazed at what your kids can do. I see this in my work with families every day. I also see the reverse, i.e., how lowered expectations results in a decline in kids' mental health: more depression, anxiety, and self-harm.

Let's go back to the two essential ingredients of setting limits: making expectations clear and holding kids accountable for meeting those expectations.

In a perfect world, all you'd need to do is set an expectation, and the kid, miraculously, would meet it. For example, let's say you notice that your teenager has a few missing homework assignments. With an easy-to-parent kid, all you might have to do is casually point this out, and the teen might say, "Yeah, I was late turning in those assignments. I'll get those done tonight." You wouldn't even need to ask them again about whether they did it because you just know they did. Super easy. Again, in a perfect world with an easy kid, there would never be a reason to give them a consequence. If they do something that's not okay, you'd talk it through, ask them not to do it again, and they wouldn't. However, if you're reading this book, that example almost seems comical because that's not your kid, is it? I bet they have lots of missing assignments, give you a huge amount of pushback on doing their homework, insist they turned it in when they didn't, and on and on. (We'll tackle homework later on.)

So, yes, kids absolutely do need consequences, and don't let anyone tell you that's not true. Simply setting a limit ("I'd like you to stay caught up on your homework") often isn't enough with a strong-willed or oppositional child. You can tell that kid over and over, until you're blue in the face, to keep up on their homework, but that isn't enough all by itself. If after setting the expectation, they don't do their homework, you're going to have a respond in a way that ensures the expectation will be met. It's the same for a younger child who keeps hitting their sibling. If telling them that there's no hitting in your family doesn't stop the hitting, you're going to need respond in a way that motivates the child to actually stop.

So, step one in behavior change is to set the limit (make the expectation clear), and step two, if the kid hasn't met the expectation, is to do or say something so that the expectation is then met. If your child curses at you for example, you must respond in a way that stops the cursing. As I said, step two is the hard part that requires a set of skills. It's easy to tell someone to cut it out, but it's much harder to get them to do it.

This is where consequences come into play. Not over-the-top, harsh or authoritarian consequences, but fair and reasonable ones. There are a couple of guiding principles to follow on this.

First, if you're going to use a consequence, you can't dole it out it out when you're angry. If you try, you're very likely going to pick a response that's both excessive and ineffective. Not every behavior requires a response from you right in that moment, and there is wisdom in taking a step back, cooling off, and then being strategic and thoughtful in your response. Whatever your child just did, there is rarely a need to come up with a consequence right then. Along these lines, you absolutely cannot use consequences to settle a score. I know your kid drives you bananas sometimes, but your response always has to be about changing their behavior for the better, and not about revenge or retaliation. Sadly, I've seen resentful parents over-consequence their kids, only to have their kids pay it back to them and then some.

Second, if you're going to give a consequence, it must be the gentlest possible consequence available that still gets the job done (ensures that the expectation has been met). Small consequences can be surprisingly effective. For example, often asking a teenager for their phone for only an hour is often (but not always) entirely sufficient to curb disrespect, and adding more time on that can be both unnecessary and counter-productive.

You might have heard something about "natural consequences." This idea has been around for a long time, and it was the big thing with kids when I first started working in mental health. It's an idea that sounds good in theory but very hard to implement in practice. Parents are encouraged to pick a consequence that fits the crime so to speak, one that is related somehow to whatever the kid did that was not okay. This is doable sometimes. For example, if you learn that your teenager is driving too fast, they might lose the privilege of driving the car for a while. That kind of natural consequence is neat and easy, but in my experience, most negative behavior isn't nearly so neat. What is a natural consequence for when your child screams at you? No clue. It's fine to pick a natural consequence if you can think of one but don't get too stuck on that. I'm going to teach you some highly effective, all-purpose consequences that aren't "natural" but still work great.

In this next chapter, I'm going to teach you how to use a particular type of consequence that is underutilized in most families (but highly effective) and help you let go of other kinds of consequences that don't work well at all.

Chief takeaways from Chapter 3

- Limit setting (making expectations of the child clear) is essential for improving the behavior of kids, especially strong-willed and oppositional kids.
- There are two steps involved in this: making the expectation clear, and, if needed, taking some kind of action to ensure that the expectation is met, i.e., a consequence of some sort.
- Keep your expectations of your child or teen high; it's good to ask a lot of them. If you lower the bar (water down your expectations), kids will hit that bar and go no higher.
- Keep the bar high even if your child has a mental health condition and do not let that become a reason for them not to meet the responsibilities of everyday life. Even kids with ADHD or whatever they have should still be asked to do their homework.
- Consequences are an important part of limit setting, but keep them kind, reasonable, and as mild as possible while still being effective.

The Art and Science of Disengaging

4

We're going to turn our attention now to another foundational skill that is going to run counter to much of the advice given in the gentle parenting community. However, I believe what follows is an essential skill, so much so that I teach it to every family raising an oppositional child or teenager prone to emotional upsets or outbursts often directed toward their parents and siblings.

The "directed toward" family here is key.

As I'm sure you know, strong-willed children and teens can get upset or highly emotional for many different reasons. Often this stems from experiencing some kind of frustration, being told "no," wanting something they can't have, being asked to do something they don't want to do, being hungry or over-tired, and much more. In my experience, all children struggle with emotion dysregulation to varying degree, some, of course, far more so than others. As kids' brains become more fully developed and with life experience, they learn how to better navigate difficult situations and get more skilled at regulating and expressing their emotions.

However, kids who are oppositional and defiant and/or kids who by temperament (traits that are more "hard wired") are more prone to emotion dysregulation, and have upsets more often and to a much larger degree. They seem to be more sensitive and need more emotional support than the average kid. In my work with families, I typically find that many of the kids who come to our clinic have siblings that don't have these same struggles—they tend just be easier-to-parent kids. Strong-willed kids are a lot harder to raise because the same skill set that works just fine with easier kids isn't as effective with them.

In my experience, oppositional kids are often really likeable and amazing in many ways, but they're just a lot harder sometimes. They didn't ask to be this way, they just are, and so the challenge for you as

DOI: 10.4324/9781003452638-6

a parent becomes how to meet your strong-willed child's emotional and behavioral needs while still fully loving and supporting them at the same time.

The gentle parenting movement has part of this exactly right. I strongly believe that an important component of being a really great parent involves being warm, paying close attention to our kids' emotional needs, being in tune with them, and in a kind and loving way helping them to navigate their bigger emotions. In addition, because these kids might be slower developmentally to acquire emotion regulations skills, they often need quite a bit more coaching and support than their easier-to-parent siblings which, as you know, can be exhausting.

It's very important to understand, however, that not all emotional upsets are the same, and the different types of upsets will require very different responses from you. Some upsetting events are best responded to by *leaning in* while others are best responded to by *leaning out*. Even If you don't learn anything else from this book, I'm hoping you'll learn this one point because it's vital to raising a child or teen who is often oppositional and prone to behavioral challenges.

Here are two examples of when and how to lean in, the first with a younger child and the second with a teenager.

Your 10-year-old is outside riding his bike with friends and the bike chain gets snagged. The bike stops abruptly and he falls off, getting scraped up. It doesn't hurt all that much, but the other kids laughing at your son hurts him a lot more and he gets mad at them. (I often find that when kids get embarrassed, they have a hard time sitting with and processing that emotion. The embarrassment then quickly turns into anger, which serves both as a smokescreen for the embarrassment, as well as a way to instead look more powerful.) Your son yells at his friends, comes home, throws his bike down in front of the house, and runs to his room crying. This would be a time, obviously, that as a parent you'd want to lean in—go to his bedroom, be soft and gentle, sit next to him on his bed, say something that's soothing and validating ("I can see why you'd be hurt and angry when your friends laughed at you, that wouldn't feel good to me either"). Most easier kids would allow you to do this and do well with this approach. You could probably offer some coaching here too, like encouraging your son to take some space in his room before going back outside, pointing out that while hurtful, the other kids probably meant no harm and it's good to be forgiving, and talk about how to go back outside and make things right with them. (And, no, I wouldn't encourage a kid that age to tell his friends how laughing at him made him feel. Ten-year-old boys just don't talk to each other that way and this would only make things worse.)

Here's an example of when to lean in with a teenager. You pick up your 16-year-old daughter from school and she asks if you can drop her off at a friend's house. She's not doing very well in school that semester, she has quite a few missing assignments, and you'd rather she came straight home to do her homework instead (a not unreasonable request, although she might disagree). You tell her this and she becomes a little frustrated, giving you all of the reasons why you should let her go and swears to you that she'll do her homework tomorrow. In this case, you would hear her out, try to understand her position, and again use some validation ("I get why you'd rather go to your friend's house instead of doing your homework"). And, your daughter handles her side of it well too—she's stays even-tempered and respectful, listens without interrupting, and either finally accepts that she can't go or you arrive at a reasonable compromise of some kind and everyone's happy.

It's really easy to stay gentle in these two examples, right? The first kid is hurting and the second is frustrated, but nothing either kid says or does is off-putting in any way. They both might be a little upset but they're still pretty well regulated, nor do they direct their hurt or anger at you and are pretty receptive to your efforts to help and talk it out.

However, in my experience with very oppositional kids, or kids who are prone to emotion dysregulation, these types of situations often don't play out as smoothly as this. Far more often, their strong negative emotions are aimed directly at their parents.

What if in these examples, both kids instead directed their anger toward you? Many oppositional and defiant kids do exactly that. In the case of the 10-year-old, what if he stormed into the house and started yelling at you, maybe even cursing at you? Or, he might blame you for what happened ("I told you I needed a new bike, why didn't you listen to me!"). You might try to point out that the bike is not all that old and the chain can be put back on, but he keeps interrupting and yelling at you. He might go to his bedroom but then escalate even more, like throwing or breaking things, maybe even punching a hole in the wall.

In the example of the teenage girl, what if she got very dysregulated and started screaming at you in the car? She might interrupt you repeatedly, tell you how unfair you are, how you don't understand, that you never let her do anything, and start cursing at you or saying very hurtful things. As soon as you get home, she escalates further and will not stop berating you.

I believe in these harder, other-directed examples, the gentle parenting advice to listen, try to understand, validate their emotions, point out better ways to handle the anger, and so on doesn't work at all, and, in fact, actually works against you.

In the face of this type of behavior, leaning in actually makes the behavior worse, not better. Why? Because we're back to the idea of reinforcement again. By allowing your child to keep and hold your attention during these upsets, to allow yourself to become the target of their anger, you're inadvertently reinforcing the very behavior you don't like. Your attention itself is often the payoff. It's also a lot easier for the kid to blame someone else when things go wrong rather than taking an honest look at their own contributions to the problem.

It can be also more than just getting attention or a chance to blame—sometimes kids have learned over time that if they keep at their parents long enough, the parent will give in and a no turns into a yes ("I finally let her go to her friend's house because I'm sick of the fighting"). Just about every parent I work with has acknowledged doing this sometimes, which is classic intermittent reinforcement. (That's when a behavior is only reinforced sometimes, unpredictably, which, according to research, is one of the most powerful ways to ensure that a behavior will keep happening.) It also reinforces the kid's persistence, i.e., it teaches them that keeping up the fight pays off. In addition, the parent finally giving in means their own behavior has been negatively reinforced (you're not getting screaming at anymore).

The other thing that happens commonly when parents stay engaged with an angry kid is what I refer to as "pinging." Pinging is when a parent says something intended to be helpful ("Well, you can see your friend this weekend") and the child or teen just gets even madder in response ("I want to see then today, not this weekend!"). For example, a kid might tell their parent that they don't love them, and when the parent reassures them that they do, the kid lights up further and might say, "Well if you loved me, you'd let me go to my friend's house!" Sometimes as parents, we ping off our kids too. We get frustrated when we keep getting unfairly blamed or hurt by something particularly mean the kid says. We'll then light up and say something that's not ideal, only to have the kid ping further in response to what we said.

And last, staying engaged with an angry disrespectful kid sends them the wrong message, i.e., that you'll still keep talking to them and trying to help no matter how horribly they're treating you. This is not how anyone else in the world is going to respond to that same behavior, so it's vital for them to learn how to deal with frustration without taking it out on other people.

I'm going to circle back to disengagement in just a moment.

Mirroring and Matching

Mirroring and matching is a very useful concept to understand and once you get the hang of it you'll find it's very helpful to put into practice, not just with kids but with adults too.

There is a natural tendency for people to mimic each other. This includes another person's facial expressions, emotional state, and their behavior, which has been extensively documented by research. This tendency is prevalent during conversations, especially conversations that have turned into an argument. The two speakers will mirror each other's emotional state, and match the volume of their voice, speaking pace, and verbal intensity. Much of this is automatic and unconscious, well outside of our awareness.

If we're having a conversation with another person, even if we disagree, and both sides stay reasonably calm, give each other the opportunity to speak without interrupting, and speak at a slow, relaxed pace, there's a good chance the conversation will perceived by both sides as a positive one. However, if one speaker becomes more emotional, starts to speak faster or with more intensity, the other speaker will unconsciously begin to mirror and match that person.

It's exactly this process that leads to heated arguments. People will "level up" during an argument, and in a step-wise fashion. The first person will start to get worked up and the second will mirror that back and match them, often leveling up further themselves (louder, faster, etc.). The first person will then match the second again and so on, often to the point where both speakers are doing nothing more than yelling at each other. Once you to begin to notice this tendency to mirror and match one another, you'll begin to see it everywhere. (Interestingly, it easier to notice other people engaging in mirroring and matching than it is yourself.) I see it happen in movies between characters all the time, and now you probably will too.

As a parent, you can capitalize on this communication dynamic and use it to your advantage with a strong-willed, reactive child.

The first thing is just to be aware of mirroring and matching when you're trying to have a conversation that has the potential to lead to conflict. If your kid starts to get angry as you're talking, try to be aware of your own urge to get angry in return. Know that if you level up, so will they, and now it's off to the races. That's why it's really important as a parent that you try to stay calm and matter-of-fact—if you can keep this up for the duration of the back and forth, it decreases the probability of a kid leveling up (not always of course).

I teach parents to go "low and slow," which means that no matter how mad or upset a kid is getting, you don't mirror them and instead do your best to stay well-regulated, not interrupt, wait a beat or two before responding (it slows the pace of the conversation down), and if you can, try not give off angry or irritated vibe as you're doing all this. I realize this will be hard at first, especially before you learn the behavior change strategies that come later in this book, but it makes it a lot harder for kids to light up and stay lit up. In addition, you're modeling for your kids that conflict in your family doesn't have to have to lead to heated arguments, or at the very least, not on your side of street.

Disengaging

So, if we know that staying engaged with a kid who is dysregulated and directing that anger at you is reinforcing them and prolonging the upset, the obvious antidote is to do the opposite: disengage.

I always advise parents that if their child or teen starts to verbally attack them (yelling, cursing, blaming, name-calling, etc.), it works best to cue them on that but only once. It sounds like this: "Hey I can't have a conversation if you're going to yell at me. Dial that back please and we can talk otherwise let's take a break." Or even more briefly: "I can't have a conversation with you when you're yelling at me." Say it once—it's important to give the kid an opportunity to do an emotional and behavioral course correct, i.e., repeat what they just said but in a nicer way. If they are able to calm down and be more respectful, stay in the conversation. (To a point that is. We'll talk about when and how to put an end to a negative, circular conversation later in the book.)

If after that one cue the kid doesn't dial it back, without a word stop speaking and walk away. Disengage and stay disengaged until the child or teen calms down (re-regulates), and is speaking you in a better way. Resist the urge to respond to anything the kid might still say to you— that's just a way for them to suck you back into an argument, i.e., to get and hold your attention again. If anything, every once in a while you can say, "I can't talk to you while you're yelling at me."

Now, I know what the gentle parenting community will say about all this. "Doesn't my child need my help to regulate their emotions? Shouldn't I be validating their feelings? They can't calm down on their own." After 40 years of successfully working with highly oppositional children and their families, I can tell you none of those statements is true. Often I'll say, "Can't regulate their emotions or doesn't regulate them?" "Can't" means the child or teen lacks the ability or capacity to do so, "doesn't" means they have the ability but they just don't do it for a variety of reasons. Evidence for "can't" versus "doesn't" can be found by looking to see if the child or teen can stay regulated and respectful in other situations or environments, like school or at a friend's house. If the behavioral upsets only occur at home (as is often the case), that's pretty good evidence that they don't control themselves rather than they can't. Now, if that same kid is having emotional upsets in most other situations or contexts too, that's a stronger argument for a capacity (a skills deficit) problem.

If the child doesn't react like that in school or other environments, they clearly have the skills to regulate their emotions and make better behavioral choices. The question becomes then why are they only having outbursts at home?

When I ask parents this question, the most common answer I hear is, "Well they hold it in at school until they get home" or "They feel safe at home." I don't think these explanations make sense. The reason I don't is because once you teach parents how to respond differently to the child's behavior when it occurs at home, in the vast majority of cases, the child's behavior improves tremendously. Here's an important take-away from this book: *How you as a parent respond to a particular behavior is largely going to determine how your kid behaves in the same situation the next time.*

There are other really good arguments for leaning away (disengaging) from kids.

Kids do need help learning how to regulate their emotions, but in my experience, very little active learning can take place with a kid who is still mad and disrespectful. I think this is true of all of us. Think about the last time you were really angry—would you have been open to skills coaching ("Maybe you should go and listen to some music?") from the person with whom you were still angry? Highly doubtful. Yet we expect kids to function differently. No, the best way to teach kids ways to handle their anger is *after they've calmed down.* And, everyone calms down eventually if you just give them enough time and space, it's a biological certainty.

By disengaging from a kid who is behaving in off-putting ways, essentially what you're saying to them is "I'll only give you my attention when you're calmer and treating me in a better way again," or "You don't get me when you're disrespectful, but I'm all in when you can express your thoughts and feelings respectfully." If your attention is what they want (the reinforcer), it's vital that you only pay attention to them again once their behavior has shifted back into a positive direction. Doing so reinforces their efforts to calm down rather than staying worked up.

I was talking to another therapist once about why it's important for a parent to disengage from a kid when they become angry and disrespectful. The therapist said to me, "Thinking as a therapist from an attachment perspective, this feels like abandonment." First, that's not abandonment. Abandonment is when you drop your kid off on a street corner and wave goodbye to them as you drive off into the sunset. Simply refusing to engage with someone when they're mistreating or even abusing you isn't abandonment, it's setting healthy boundaries on the relationship. Second, this is exactly what people do in their adult relationships. If your spouse or partner got so angry that they started scream at you and say horrible things, you'd walk away from them (and if you didn't walk away from them, I promise your therapist would tell you to do exactly that).

You're not abandoning your child or damaging your attachment by walking away. You're still the same loving, kind, supportive parent ready and willing to fully engage again but not while the kid is mistreating you.

In our clinic, my colleagues and I work oppositional, often destructive kids who engage in this behavior, sometimes on daily basis. At the start of treatment, I'll gather a history and ask a parent to describe the last time their child was really upset and how they responded to it (what the parent said or did while the child was mad at them). I had one father of an eight-year-old tell me this:

> 'Well, first I would tell her over and over to stop but that just seems to make her even madder. I'll tell her to go to her room to calm down, but she usually doesn't go until I take her by the arm. By that time, she's hitting and kicking me. Once I get her to her bedroom, I'll go inside with her, shut the door, and keep my back against it so she can't leave (otherwise she'll go after everyone else in the house). She'll start throwing things at me and I tell her to stop. I ask her why she's mad but she doesn't know or blames me somehow. This can go on for an hour or even longer. Eventually she asks me to read or sing to her (she demands it and won't stop until I do) and then she finally calms down. This happens almost every day."

Uh-oh. Okay, so we can see what's going on here. The dad is obviously very well intentioned, but it's clear that his own behavior is reinforcing his daughter's negative behavior. He's sending her the message "When you freak out, you have my undivided attention." The first thing we do with a family in this situation is teach parents about reinforcement (what gets reinforced, gets repeated) and explain why going to the girl's bedroom and sitting with her is what is actually maintaining her out-of-control episodes ("feeding the dragon"). She's learned over time that one of the best ways to get and hold her dad's attention is by having these big upsets, i.e., her upsets have been positively reinforced. By the dad sitting with his daughter in her room, he's reinforcing the very behavior he doesn't care for but he doesn't realize it (and of course neither does she). The dad has also learned over time that sitting with her in her bedroom "is the only thing that works," so his behavior has been negatively reinforced (he gets relief because the tantrum stops).

This is the most common mistake I see parents make with oppositional and easily dysregulated kids—they give them attention during upsets rather than giving their attention only when the child has calmed down. This is a younger kid example but I see the same dynamic play out with teenagers. With teenagers, they'll get really angry and disrespectful, and they are masters at keeping their parents engaged in a heated back and forth.

Disengaging is the antidote to this unhelpful reinforcement pattern. "*I can't have a conversation with you while you're yelling at me. Happy to talk once you've calmed down.*"

It is very important that you never have a back and forth with a kid who is yelling at you or calling you names. Don't ask them how they're feeling (that's obvious isn't it?), why they're doing it (they have no idea), don't try to "process" their emotions, or think it's your job in that moment to help them calm down.

In truth, it's the child or teen's job to calm themselves down. And it's important that kids not get the message that they need others to help them calm down or that they have become dependent on other people to make that happen. By withdrawing your attention, the child will be motivated to calm themselves down, and each upset is an opportunity for them to practice doing so. Every time you stay engaged with an angry kid, you are denying them the opportunity to learn how to calm themselves down.

A question I'm asked often is how long will it take for their child's behavior to start improving (fewer, briefer, and less intense upsets) once the parent gets in the habit of walking away from a kid who becomes angry and disrespectful? That varies quite a bit, but probably a good ballpark is several weeks to a few months. It certainly doesn't happen overnight. Remember, this pattern of reinforcement has often been in place with most families for years, so it's going to take some time for the new reinforcement pattern (walking away followed by only giving attention when the child has calmed down) to do its job.

In my experience, it's slow going at first, and in fact it often initially makes things worse temporarily. Kids are accustomed to getting their parent's attention via these upsets, and when you begin to withdraw your attention, they will often pull harder for it. This is what's known as an "extinction burst," i.e., a temporary burst of even more negative behavior once the reinforcement for it has been withdrawn. So buckle up. However, in most cases, the frequency and intensity of upsets begins to slowly reduce. Emotional upsets and other-directed behavior will often be reduced to zero or close to it, but expect that it may still pop up again from time to time. Don't be surprised or discouraged if it does, that's pretty normal. Sometimes when this happens a parent will tell me "Now we're back to square one." No you're not, the kid just had a bad day, as we all do from time to time.

It's important to know too that while disengaging is essential, that alone is probably not going be enough for this behavior to stop with many strong-willed kids. You'll likely need to pair disengaging with other incentives that we will get to in the later chapters of this book.

As I said, learning and skill building take place after an event, not during it. It works best for parents to circle back to upsets with the child once they've fully calmed down, often the next day. That's where the best teaching can happen. I recommended that families circle back routinely after a big event to make full use of these teaching moments, as well as to create a culture in the family where upsets can be talked about, not swept under the rug.

The conversation flows like this:

PARENT (P):   Come here for a second, would you? I want to have a quick conversation with you about something.

CHILD (C):   Am I in trouble?

(P):   No, but I want to talk about the other day.

(C):   What about it?

(P):   Well, remember when we were driving home together and you got really upset? What was that all about?

(C):   What do you mean?

(P):   You started yelling at me and called me names.

(C):   That's because you made me mad.

(P):   How so?

(C):   Because I asked to go to my friend's house and you told me I couldn't. You never let me do anything. *[Note: "You never let me do anything" is what I call a red herring. It's best to never respond to a red herring—more on this later in the book.]*

(P):   I know it's frustrating when you want to do something and I tell you you can't but what does that have to do with calling me a name?

[I think both the wording of this and the message itself are very important. A lot of kids will say this—you made me mad therefore I did x, y, and z. They say that as if it's an explanation, that cursing (or damaging property, being disrespectful, hitting, etc.) is an inevitability of being mad. It isn't. I tell kids they can be mad, or have whatever feeling they're having, but having an emotion doesn't mean the behavior that follows it is okay. Feelings are a part of being human, but cursing at someone isn't okay no matter how mad they are.]

(C):   I get mad and I can't help it.

(P):   Look, here's the thing. If you're mad, be mad. But you know that cursing at me, no matter how mad you are, isn't okay. We don't curse at each other in our family. And, can I ask you, did that work, you calling me a hurtful name?

(C):   What do you mean?

(P):   I mean, did you get to go to your friend's house after you cursed at me?

(C):   No, obviously.

(P).   Exactly. You'll never get something from me when you say those things to me. What might you have tried instead?

(C):   Nothing. You weren't going to let me go.

(P):   Maybe, but I'm not sure about that. You might have tried negotiating with me. And staying being nice while you did it. Soft and gentle always works better with me. That's not a guarantee that I'll always say yes, sometimes a no is a no, but you're far more likely to get what you want if you at least try in a nice way. Does that make sense?

(C):   I guess.

(P):   I love you. But we're not always going to agree on everything, and sometimes we might get mad at each other. That's just being human, but next time let's try to disagree in a more loving way.

I'd stop the conversation here and leave it at that. It's vital that this not sound like a lecture, and if the conversation goes beyond just a few minutes, kids are going to stop listening, and you'll just end up rehashing the same ideas. Short and sweet.

However, if this is a kid who was in the habit of cursing at me, I'd for sure give them a consequence or penalty of some kind that has been established and agreed upon in advance. I said earlier that talking things through and setting limits in a gentle way is essential, but sometimes that's insufficient (necessary, but not enough). We'll get to some reasonable and effective consequences in just a bit.

Okay, so never have a conversation with an angry, disrespectful kid. Disengage. And when you disengage, try to adopt a matter-of-fact demeanor when you do. Disengaging with an angry vibe isn't helpful. Just go about your business whatever that is. Parents set the tone for the house—if there are other kids or adults at home try to set an upbeat tone and interact with them as you normally would. Try not to let the child's angry mood become contagious for the rest of the house, which often occurs. I think of an angry, disrespectful kid as "vibrating"—no need for you to vibrate with them (and it prolongs their upset if you do).

I also find it helpful not to re-engage with the kid first—it works much better to wait for them to come to you. As I said, all kids calm down eventually, usually within an hour or two, occasionally longer. When they do try to re-engage you and if they seem fully back on track, warm right up and say something like "I appreciate you calming down and talking to me the way you are right now." Don't hold a grudge or freeze kids out after they've calmed own; it's back to family life as usual.

It's important to know that some kids do not allow their parents to disengage. They can do that in a variety of ways, such as following their parents around the house and still saying mean things. Or they'll up the ante in some way hoping you'll re-engage, i.e., they'll try to find some behavior that's a lot harder for you to ignore, like tormenting a sibling or breaking something. I worked with a family whose 13-year-old daughter would go to great lengths to re-engage her parents, such as taking a knife to the furniture. My advice to them? Don't engage. I know that's hard, but she'd do this every time because now she knew it worked. (I asked the parents just to leave the house when she escalated like this, and, not surprisingly, the upsets stopped immediately as soon as they left). We also built in all kinds of other penalties and incentives to address the property destruction, which were highly effective, so much so that the outbursts stopped completely.

Most kids don't go as far as cutting up furniture but if yours does you're going to need professional help to implement this part. I work with quite a few kids who threaten self-harm if their parents try to disengage. This exact strategy works with this too—in our clinic we do it all the time—but as I said in the introduction, whenever safety becomes a concern do not attempt this on your own, and instead find a therapist who can walk you through the process.

Remember, as I said earlier in the book, kids don't feel good about behaving this way, and most of them feel really bad about it once they've calmed down. Sometimes, just teaching kids skills they can use when they're angry is helpful, but in my experience, that alone rarely works. Nothing changes until the reinforcement patterns change.

I know your instincts as a parent are to lean in and soothe your child when they're upset, and all of this might go against the grain for you somewhat, at least at first, but that just doesn't work well when the angry upsets are directed at you. Give your child time and space to calm down so they can practice regulating their own emotions, but then once they do lean in fully and completely—affectionate, loving, and gentle—full steam ahead.

Chief takeaways from Chapter 4

- The gentle parenting movement encourages parents to lean into kids' emotional upsets by listening to them, validating their feelings, helping them process their strong emotions, and teaching new skills. Leaning in is a great approach when those feelings and behaviors aren't being directed outwardly toward others in a negative way.

- However, leaning in will often backfire with strong-willed kids under certain circumstances.

- If a child or teen is directing their negative emotions and behaviors toward you (disrespect, unkind comments, blaming you, and so on), remaining in a conversation with them will often make those behaviors worse over time.

- In that situation, leaning out (disengaging) is much more helpful. It is important for kids to be given opportunities to regulate their emotions and behavior without your help, and for them to know they can't get and hold your attention if they are being unkind.

- Mirroring and matching is the tendency for people in conversation, especially when in conflict, to mirror each other's emotional state, and to match the other person's speaking volume, pace and intensity. This is helpful to know because conversations with strong-willed kids can often escalate, so going "low and slow" makes it less likely interactions will spin out of control. It also decreases the chances of "pinging," saying something you believe is helpful but only makes the kid madder.

- Learning and skill building won't take place while kids are still angry and actively engaging in off-putting, negative behavior. However, once kids have calmed down and are back on track, circling back and having a conversation about skills and better ways to handle their emotions can be very effective.

Better Communication with a Lot Less Conflict **5**

Never Argue with Your Kid Again (Really!)

Here's the truth of it: kids are notoriously good at arguing with their parents. However, a lesser-acknowledged fact is that parents are equally good at arguing with their kids.

This is a purposefully outrageous statement that I make to parents at the start of treatment, which they never believe at first: *You never need to have another argument with your child or teen again*. A conversation, sure, but an argument, no. An argument, by definition, is when two people are speaking, usually with the aim or purpose of convincing the other person of something. If one person simply stops speaking, by definition, it's no longer an argument. At that point, it's just one person up on a soap box giving a speech or a monologue, albeit a long and passionate one sometimes, but it's definitely no longer an argument.

As parents, we get sucked into a back-and-forth argument with our kids all the time. As James Lehman once said, "You don't have to attend every argument you're invited to." Let's take a look at and dissect the anatomy of an argument and what you can do to sidestep them with your kid.

Let Go of Persuasion

This is the first unhelpful contributor that parents make to having arguments with their kids. We try so hard to convince our kids of something— why they should do their homework, take out the trash, be nice to their sibling, get off their phones or gaming systems, and so on. I think we believe this is just a part of parenting, i.e., teaching our kids the value or importance of doing things. We hold out hope that if we just say *the right words*, our kids will understand and agree with us.

DOI: 10.4324/9781003452638-7

When has this ever happened to you (or anyone for that matter?) After an hour long, heated argument with your kid about why it's important for them to do their homework, do they finally see the light and say in a sincere, nonsarcastic way, *"Oh my God, now I'm finally understanding! What was I thinking? Of course I should be doing my homework! You've been telling me this for years, why didn't I listen? Mom and Dad, you were right, as always. Thank you so much!"*

Ain't gonna happen.

Kids just don't work this way (and neither do adults for that matter). Here's what is also true: when a person is highly incentivized (motivated) not to understand something, they're not going to understand it no matter how sound your reasoning or how persuasive you are. As the novelist Upton Sinclair put it, "It's difficult to get a man to understand something when his salary depends on not understanding it."

No kid wants to do chores, homework, clean their room, or put down their phone. A little persuasion from you might be helpful, sure, as it's always best I think to offer some simple rationale for asking something of a kid. The "Do it because I said so" approach from the past, while tempting, is too far in the authoritarian direction. But, how much explanation is really needed for why a kid should be doing their homework? It's pretty straightforward so treat it as such—no need to ever do a long back and forth on obvious and self-evident tasks or responsibilities. This is just a trap to keep you in a circular exchange that very likely will only leave you feeling frustrated and probability even a little confused.

Tug-Of-Wars

We've all either seen or played this game on the beach: two groups of people line up in opposite directions and pull as hard on a long rope as they can to drag the other team over a line in the center. Each team tries its best to win so they pull as hard as possible, which then causes the other team to pull back with equal force, resulting in a stalemate that can go on for some time.

Every time you try to persuade your child or teen of something that in turn they resist, you're in a tug-of-war. You're both pulling equally hard on that rope, hoping that you'll pull the other over some imaginary line. Remember too that your kid is highly incentivized to pull back just as hard on that rope—not to do their homework, put down their phone, or clean their room. They've potentially a lot to lose here, so it's in their best interests to argue with you hoping to persuade you or wear you down (or at least buy themselves some time to avoid doing what was asked of them). That's why they will argue with you endlessly, or for whatever amount of time you'll give them. This scenario is often one that results in mirroring and matching, i.e., the step-wise increase in heat and negatively that results in a full-blown argument.

The most effective way to avoid a tug-of-war with your child or teen is to *let go of the rope.* As soon as you stop pulling (persuading or convincing), the kid loses all incentive to keep pulling back in return. The goal isn't to win the battle, it's to stop the game.

Here's an example of letting go of the rope. In the treatment model that I've developed, Intensive Family-Focused Therapy, we routinely video record all of our family therapy sessions. I recall watching a session in which the conversation turned to the teenage boy falling far behind on his homework assignments. This was by far not the first time it had happened. There were several instances in the past in which he had accumulated quite a few missing assignments, but he insisted that he be allowed to be independent on his homework. He didn't want his parents to add any structure to his homework routine (or, more accurately, his lack of routine), such as asking him to do his homework as soon as he got home after school, keep his devices off each day until his homework was done, and so on. Every time they would agree to letting him get his homework done on his own, he wouldn't do it, and each time they put structure in place he would.

The session I observed was during one of those time that he had talked them out of imposing structure, so quite predictably he had many missing assignments. Not but a few minutes into the conversation, the family got into a massive tug-of-war over homework. The parents started by explaining why they were going to go back to the daily structure and their reasons for doing so, and the boy gave them all of the reasons he didn't want them to do that. This went on for a full 45 minutes. This particular boy was really good at sucking his parents into pointless arguments (and they had a hard time seeing when they were in one), and he was in no hurry whatsoever to stop pulling on that homework rope.

Finally, one of the parents realized what was going on. They quite nicely let go of the rope by saying, "Well, we're not going to argue with you. We'd like you to do your homework right after school every day and once done we'd be happy to turn on your phone." The boy tried to argue again and they just said, "I'm sorry you don't agree but we're done talking about this." That was it—he kept trying to argue for a few minutes but they said nothing in response, and eventually the conversation turned to a different subject.

Let go of the rope. Make your point, hear the kid out for a few minutes, set the limit ("Here's how we're doing homework from now on"), and disengage. And I do mean hear them out for just a few minutes. As I said earlier, kids will take whatever time you give them to talk you out of something, and the longer you let it go on, the more creative and persuasive their arguments will become. Most conversations that include limit setting can be done in under just a minute or two because anything longer than that increases the chances of a tug-of-war and a possible escalation.

No Lecturing Either Please

Kids will monologue, sure, but parents often do too. A lecture is when a parent gives a lengthy, repetitive, often one-sided explanation (parent talks and the kids listens) as to why something is so. Again, I think the temptation to lecture comes from the fact that as parents we see it as our duty to convince kids of things, so we have the urge to do the convincing as long as we can get away with it, and from as many angles as possible, hoping that the lesson sticks. Lecturing is bit of a power move too—insisting that a kid sit in silence while you talk at them is an unnecessary display of dominance and control.

The problem is kids hate lectures. In most cases too, lectures just make kids mad and if you're lucky enough that they don't blow up at you in the middle of it or walk away, instead they'll just completely tune you out.

I once worked with a really likeable, super smart 11-year-old. He was very creative and would build all kinds of cool science and engineering projects in his garage. Some of these projects were quite hazardous, involving strange chemicals at very high temperatures, so, naturally, he would sometimes get in trouble with his dad. Unfortunately, the dad was very prone to giving long lectures, often lasting upwards of half an hour. He also leaned heavily in the authoritarian direction, so it wasn't smart for the boy to do anything other than just listen to the lecture. I asked him what he did for those 30 minutes, how he passed the time, and this is what he said, "Well I mostly say nothing because if I do anything other than agree the lecture will just go on longer. Every so often I'll say 'That's true, Dad' or 'You're right, Dad, I'm sorry.' He likes that. But the rest of the time I just think about random stuff, my homework, what's for dinner, or whatever until it's over."

Was the dad right that it was dangerous for the boy to mix chemicals and fire in the garage? For sure. However, the way he tried to keep this from happening again (lecturing) was ineffective. A little later in the book I'll talk about making if/then statements, which have worked much better with this kid (or any kid for that matter).

Red Herrings

As I mentioned previously, strong-willed kids are really good at arguing with their parents. Often, when we ask a kid to do something that they don't want to do, they throw what I call red herrings at you in an attempt not to do thing that's been asked.

A red herring is an attempt at distraction, a comment that's made by a kid that loosely relates to the request made of them with the hopes of talking their parents out of it, or at least stalling as long as possible. The best way to teach how red herrings work is to give you an example:

PARENT (P): The lawn is looking like it needs to be mowed. Can you take care of that?

CHILD (C): I did it last time so it's not my turn.

(P): No, your brother did it last time, I think.

(C): That was the time before.

(P): Pretty sure it is your turn. Plus, he's not home right now.

(C): He can do it when he gets home.

(P): I'm not sure when he's getting back. Please just do it, okay?

(C): Why does he do less around here than me? You make me do everything.

(P): He doesn't do less than you. The chores are equal.

(C): Mine are a lot harder than his. You guys always give me the harder chores. That's not fair.

(P): He has some harder chores too. Just mow the lawn.

(C): No, he doesn't. Tell me what hard chores he has?

(P): I don't know. Why do you always do this?

(C): The lawn mower won't start anyway. You were supposed to fix it last time so I can't do it.

(P): I did fix it.

(C): Then how come it doesn't start?

You can see where this is going, right? Exactly nowhere. Everything the kid said in that example is a red herring. It's just designed to pull the parent off course and frustrate them, hoping to delay or even get out of mowing the lawn (or even better still from their perspective, the parent ends up mowing the lawn to avoid a fight). In my experience, many easily succumb to red herrings. The worst thing you can do when your kid throws a red herring at you is to respond to the red herring itself (offer a counter argument), which is exactly what this parent did. Doing so just turns the conversation into a nonsensical back and forth, similar to a tug-of-war. Once you know what a red herring is and get good at spotting them, it becomes quite liberating because they become almost comical, and you can sidestep them easily.

The best way to sidestep a red herring is to use words like nonetheless, nevertheless, regardless, in any case, be that as it may, and so on. They all mean basically the same thing. In the lawn example, it would go like this:

(P):   The lawn is looking like it needs to be mowed. Can you take care of that?

(C):   I did it last time.

(P):   Well, nonetheless, it needs doing please.

(C):   That's not fair, it's not my turn.

(P):   In any case, I'd like you to do it please.

(C):   I do everything around here.

(P):   Be that as it may, I'm not going to argue with you. It's needs to be done please.

[This is the point in which you'd go silent. This is obviously not a real conversation about fairness, or whether chores have been assigned equally. It goes without saying that you should be fair about dividing chores between siblings and not favoring one kid over another. If your child or teen has a valid point about this, then obviously address the concern, but in most cases this is just an obvious red herring.]

You can see what words like nonetheless and regardless do—they completely sidestep the red herring (the actual content of what the kid is saying) and go right back to your essential point, "Mow the lawn please."

Once you say, "I'm not going to argue with you," you have to mean it and actually not argue. Now, of course, this doesn't mean the kid will actually mow the lawn (I'll teach you how to get kids to do their chores later in the book), but this approach will save you many heated arguments. You'll need to practice not arguing over and over (for months probably), but once your child or teenager learns that you've stopped arguing with them, they will gradually fall out of the habit of trying to suck you into these endless and frustrating conversations.

Gray and Yellow Rocks

The idea here is that sometimes with strong-willed and oppositional kids it is best again to simply not argue with them and using a gray or yellow rock strategy can be an effective way to keep yourself from doing so. Gray and yellow rock are mostly the same idea but there is a slight difference between the two, so you can choose whichever one best fits your needs in the moment.

The term gray rock is attributed to a blogger who goes by the name Skylar. In 2012, Skylar wrote that a gray rock was the most boring, uninteresting thing that came to mind. Metaphorically, a gray rock is something heavy and immovable; it just sits there and there's not much anyone can do about it. Gray rock is a way to respond to someone in a matter-of-fact, unemotional way in situations that otherwise might lead to unnecessary conflict or upset.

It's best to use a gray-rock response when you're firm about ending a conversation and clearly communicating to the child or teen that negotiating with you or badgering is not an option.

Here are some examples of gray rock:

> "I'm not going to argue with you and this conversation is over."
> "You can't see your friends this weekend until your room is cleaned up—that's always the rule."
> "Homework comes before time on your phone or gaming. It's that way every day."
> "We don't curse or say mean things to each other in our family."

You can see how final and certain each one of these sounds. That's the message you're trying to send to the kid, i.e., that you simply won't argue and the conversation is over. (Usually after making a gray rock statement it's best to turn around and walk away, further signaling that the conversation is over.) Notice too that none of these examples ends in an exclamation point. Gray rock is just as it sounds—matter-of-fact, firm, and final, and in as bored a tone as you can muster.

Sometimes I see parents make an attempt at a gray rock statement but they give off a very timid vibe, sound uncertain, and might even put an "okay?" at the end ("Homework comes before gaming, okay?"). All of that dilutes the effectiveness of gray rock, and the "okay" at the end almost implies that the kid must give consent for them to follow the rule or the expectation. Of course, it's important to give your kids a say in things whenever you reasonably can, especially as they get older, but you do not need their consent to treat you nicely, do their homework, clean their room, and any other responsibilities of life.

The term yellow rock was coined by Tina Swithin, and it's a bit of a variation on this same idea. A yellow rock, as the name implies, is still a rock but it has a bit more warmth to it. Where a gray rock statement is firm and with emotion removed on purpose to convey seriousness or finality, yellow rock adds just a bit of validation and warmth at the beginning but still firmly holds the line on whatever the limit or expectation is that you're trying to establish.

I'll use the same gray rock examples but turn them into more of a yellow-rock statement:

> "Look, I know this is important to you, I get that, but I'm not going to argue with you and the conversation is over."
>
> "No one is excited to have to clean their room, but you know that you can't see your friends until it's done—that's just the family rule."
>
> "Who wants to do homework? I'm sure you'd rather be doing almost anything else. Homework always comes first though before time on your phone or gaming."
>
> "I understand that sometimes you get frustrated and angry, but we don't curse or say mean things to each other in our family."

As a general rule, I'd probably lean more toward a gray rock response if it seemed clear to me that the kid was just in an argumentative frame of mind and I felt like they were being unkind or disrespectful to me. I'd for sure want to bring that to a quick close. However, I'd probably use a yellow-rock response if I felt like the kid wasn't being overtly disrespectful. If they were just frustrated or upset about the situation or the request itself without directing that anger toward me, then yellow rock would be the better response.

Ask Not Command

This is a really cool technique that will increase the probability of your child or teen following through on a request to do something. I'm sure if you're reading this book, you've got a kid who struggles with following directions, so often even simple requests can become a battle. Daily life might even feel like never-ending conflict, which is no fun for you or them. We're going to talk later in the book about how to get strong-willed, oppositional kids to follow directions, but ask not command is more of a communication strategy that increases the probability of compliance and lays the foundation for other techniques that I'm going to teach you.

The idea behind here is that the way we speak to kids and ask them to do something goes a long way in either increasing the probability that they'll do it or decrease it. Often, our tone of voice and how the sentence is constructed can play a major role in whether a kid will follow directions or fight them.

There is a natural evolution that takes place in how we ask kids to do something as they age. I don't think we even have an awareness of how our language begins to shift over time, but in my work with families I have observed that sometimes parents can be slow to make the developmental shift, resulting in conflict that is often avoidable.

Here's how all of this works.

When kids are little, say up until the age of 10 or so, we most often make a request that is worded much more like a command instead of an ask. A command is just a straightforward way of wording a directive, something like "Please go get your pajamas on and then brush your teeth," "Get started on your homework," or "The dog needs to be fed." The thing about younger kids is that they accept directives worded in this way fairly well, and while they might not follow the direction from time to time, they generally don't respond negatively to how the directive itself is worded. We "command" little kids to do things all the time and it feels right both to us and to them.

However, as kids get older, especially as they move into adolescence, they become much more sensitive to power imbalances and the importance of not losing face. They become much more prickly in response to directives worded as commands and become far more likely to resist them. Often, parents still see their kids as younger versions of themselves and continue to speak to them in a way that is more consistent with a younger child.

The alternative to a command is an "ask." An ask is what is called "mitigated speech," a term used by linguists popularized by the author

Malcom Gladwell in his book *Outliers*. Mitigated speech is when you phrase something in a way that softens the meaning of what you're saying (it's less direct) so that it minimizes power imbalances and conveys respect. For example, if two adults are driving somewhere and they're a little confused as to which way to turn, the passenger might point and say, "I'm wondering if we should be headed in that direction?" rather than telling the driver "You need to go that way."

Adults often use mitigated speech with each other because we've learned that in most instances (besides in the military or other organizations with a clear chain of command) this is a more deferential, respectful way of asking someone to do something that still leaves the meaning clear. Another example would be I might say to my wife something like, "This might be a good weekend for us to clean out the garage." My meaning is clear (we should clean out the garage this weekend) but by phrasing it the way I did, I've conveyed respect and collaboration. Instead, if I had said, "We're cleaning out the garage this weekend" (a command), my wife would have (correctly) interpreted this as an order and responded negatively.

Kids, especially older ones, don't like being given orders any more than my wife does. The problem is we do it all of the time, likely because we've been slow developmentally to transition from a command to an ask. Asking works so much better with older kids because they perceive it as respectful—that's how they see adults speak to each other after all.

Here are some examples of how to turn a command into an ask:

Command	Ask
It's time to feed the dog.	The dog looks hungry. Before you get started doing your homework would you mind feeding her please? Thanks for taking care of that.
Come out here and empty the dishwasher.	I'd love it if you could come and empty the dishwasher in the next few minutes, please. Thanks so much.
Take your shoes to your room.	Hey, on your way down to your room, would you be kind enough to take your shoes with you? That'd be super helpful thanks.
When family comes over this afternoon, no hiding out in your room	I'd love it if when family comes over today if you could hang out and make conversation for a while. It would mean a lot to them and to me. Thanks very much.

"I'd love it if you could …?" "Would you mind …?" This is exactly how adults word something when speaking to each other, and you can see how phrasing it this way would land better with almost anyone.

Sometimes when I explain ask not command to parents they'll say "Am I really asking them if they'll empty the dishwasher? Doesn't that make it sound like emptying the dishwasher is optional?" No, not really. Remember, the meaning of mitigated speech is still clear, the phrasing is just softened and stretched out a bit. If a kid refuses to empty the dishwasher, you'll follow the steps that come later in the book to ensure that they do. It's very important that you make sure your kids do everything you ask of them otherwise they will come to believe that your requests are optional. Here's what will happen: if you fall out of the habit of giving commands and into the habit of making asks, your kids will come to understand that the wording is different, but the expectation is still the same. Ask not command increases the probability of compliance, it doesn't decrease it.

You likely noticed the "thanks for taking care of that" in each of these examples. It's obviously good to be polite when you talk to your kids (or anyone else) but including the thank you is more than that. At first glance, it might seem odd to thank someone for doing something that they haven't actually done yet. I can't explain why this works, I just know that it does. Maybe there's something about being thanked in advance that makes the other person feel obligated to return the favor. In his book, *Influence: The Psychology if Persuasion*, the social psychologist Robert Cialdini talks about the concept of reciprocity. He argues that people are wired to pay back debts and return favors, so perhaps "thanks for taking care of that" creates an incentive for a kid to return the favor by doing what was asked of them.

I'm going to close out our discussion of ask not command with a story that highlights this idea nicely. I watched a family therapy session in which a 13-year-old girl wanted to bring up something with her father that had occurred a few days prior. She'd been in her bedroom when he walked in for some reason. He noticed a big pile of dishes on her dresser, and, as is the case with many parents, there was a rule in the family that she not let dirty dishes pile up in her room. He got angry pretty quickly, likely because he'd asked her many times to stop doing this. So far he had been unable to change her behavior, and so yelled, "Get these dishes out of your room and into the kitchen where they belong!" Clearly, this was a command.

So, in the session, here's what she said to her father:

"I shouldn't have left my dishes in my room that's true. But here's what I don't understand. Why did you have to give me an order? I've seen you talk to your friends and you don't order them around. You ask them nicely to do something for you. And it's the same with Mom—I've never seen you give her an order. If you're in the living room and she's in the kitchen and you want her to bring you something, you ask if she wouldn't mind bringing it to you. Why do you feel it's okay to order you just because I'm a kid?"

Amen to her.

Chief takeaways from Chapter 5

- You never need to argue with your child or teen, ever. I know this probably sounds like an impossibility or a dream come true, but I promise you it can be done. You don't have to attend every argument your kid invites you to.
- A little bit of persuasion (your reason for asking something of a kid) is good, but anything more than a little is counter-productive and likely will lead to more resistance.
- A tug-of-war is a back-and-forth argument whereby you try hard to convince your child to do something, and they pull back with equal force to convince you why they shouldn't. If you find yourself in a tug-of-war, it's best let go of the rope and stop trying to convince them and instead just set the expectation and walk away.
- Lecturing kids is not helpful. They just tune you out and wonder what's for dinner.
- Be on the lookout for red herrings, i.e., arguments kids will throw at you in an attempt not to do something. Don't ever respond to a red herring; instead, you can easily sidestep them by using words like nonetheless or regardless.
- Using a gray or yellow rock response can put an end to most arguments. Gray rock is when you're matter-of-fact and firm ("The rule is clean your room first and then you can use your tablet"). Yellow rock is similar, but you add a little warmth and validation ("I know you really hate having to clean your room, I get that. But it's always room first, tablet second."
- As kids get older, they become very sensitive to being given orders ("Clean up your room"). What works far better than a command is an ask, whereby you soften your language as you would if you were speaking with another adult while still keeping the meaning clear, such as "Before we leave for the movies today, I'd love it if you could clean up your room. Thanks for taking care of that."

Part III

Tools for Lasting Behavior Change

Ways to Use Positive Reinforcement that Work

6

Here are the communication strategies that we've covered so far, which I've argued are essential to being able to best parent a strong-willed child or teen.

- Getting good at limit setting and having high behavioral expectations of your child.
- Disengaging and walking away when your child becomes angry and escalated.
- Understanding and counteracting the principle of mirroring and matching.
- Avoiding communication traps such as arguing, persuading, red herrings, and tug-of-wars, and use alternative communication strategies such as gray and yellow rocks and ask not command.

I have one more foundational strategy that we're going to cover here: ways to use positive reinforcement that you might not be doing now.

Positive Reinforcement

Research has consistently shown that positive reinforcement is a very powerful change strategy for all kinds of different behaviors, and not just for kids. For example, if you've ever taught a dog to sit or shake, you know that's all done through the use of positive reinforcement. You start by saying the word sit, and of course the dog looks at you and has no idea what you're talking about. However, if you say it and wait a few moments, most dogs will eventually sit all on their own. You then give him a treat paired with a really enthusiastic "good boy!" The dog still hasn't figured out what any of this means, but if you pair the command

DOI: 10.4324/9781003452638-9

and the treat again and again, he finally gets the hang of it. You can eventually withdraw the treat altogether and the dog will still sit, but you'll probably keep the "good boy!" in place so there's still a little positive reinforcement going on.

I feel strongly that any effective strategy to improve the behavior of oppositional kids must include the regular use of positive reinforcement. There are so many ways of doing this but the first step involves noticing when a kid did something you want them to do more often, or didn't do something negative in a situation in which they might have made a bad decision but didn't. When this happens, the next step is doing or saying something that the kid likes that increases the probability of them doing it again. We covered the basics of positive reinforcement in Chapter 2 so I won't go into them again, and there are lots of online resources and books you can access that talk about things like sticker charts or a fun outing for younger kids, or extra privileges such as more time on the computer, a later bedtime, and so on for older kids.

The Problem with Positive Reinforcement for Oppositional Kids

Here's what I've learned from my work with families who have kids who are challenging: positive reinforcement is very often in short supply.

It's not hard to understand why—these kids are challenging. They frequently get into trouble and drive their parents up the wall. There is often so much conflict, negativity, and bad feelings that parents feel they have few or no opportunities to reinforce any kind of positive behavior ("We don't even get a chance because they're always in trouble for something"). This creates a cycle of negativity between the parent and the kid: the kid does something they're not supposed to do, and the parent calls them out on it, over and over. As a parent of an oppositional child or teen, you probably know that they don't respond particularly well to being criticized or corrected, even when you're fully justified for doing so. Most of the time, the kid gets angry and defensive, and then, they usually blame their behavior on you or someone else. In response, many parents get angrier and even more critical, and so on.

Over time, this cycle of negativity often becomes pervasive and entrenched, which results in family members becoming increasingly hurt and resentful of one another. Parents pull back emotionally because they've been burned so many times, and the kid feels like they can't do anything right because in their mind they're always getting criticized and punished. The kid and the parents become increasingly disconnected from one another over time, which only adds more fuel to the fire. When this type of disconnection takes root, I believe this is very painful for kids and only serves to incentivize them further to keep breaking rules. They begin to see themselves as bad kids, after all they're in trouble almost every day, so they start to move through the world proving this negative self-image to others again and again. Call a dog by a new name and they will eventually answer to it. This must be who I am.

Eventually, a lot of emotional space develops between the kid and the parent due to all of the behavioral challenges that have occurred and sit in between them, leaving little room for any kind of positivity and mutual warmth. This is usually the point at which families come to my clinic—everyone has retreated to their separate corners until it's time to come out and spar again. No one likes the situation but no one knows how to change it. I often ask parents newly in treatment when the last time was that their family was playful and silly with each other, or just laughing and having fun. This is often a painful question for them, which elicits a great deal of sadness as it becomes clear just how far off course the family has become.

I feel a large part of my job as a family therapist is to reduce the emotional space that sits between kids and their parents, and to reconnect them again. However, behavior problems must be solved first or the disconnection and negativity will remain. Who can be close when there's conflict, upsets, and bad feelings every day?

I've learned that when a child or teen's behavior improves, the cycle of negativity reverses itself and positive interactions become the norm. I always know I'm close to being done with a family when they can spend the session laughing and being playful with each other.

I find that it is an interesting and useful exercise to ask parents this question: What percentage of the time do you feel your kid is actively misbehaving—doing or saying something that they're not supposed to? I generally get very high percentages as you might guess: 50%, 70%, or "pretty much all the time." I spent many years working directly with kids who couldn't live at home due to the severity of their behavior problems and I can tell you that even the hardest kids I ever worked with probably actively misbehaved only maybe 5% of the time. The vast majority of the time they were doing exactly what they were supposed to be doing, or at the very least their behavior was pleasantly neutral.

No matter what number the parent comes up with I'll subtract it from 100. "Well, if they're misbehaving 50% of the time, that means 50% of the time they're doing something you can reinforce." I often use the term *opportunities for reinforcement,* a chance to notice something the kid did right and call them out for it in a positive way.

For example, let's say your child wants to do something and for whatever reason you have to say no. Normally, they might not take this very well and would likely get mad, argue, grind you down to turn your no into a yes, and so on. But, on this one occasion for who knows what reason, they actually accept the no pretty well. That's an opportunity for reinforcement—an unexpected chance to do or say something to reinforce their positive behavior.

I've heard people talk about ratios quite a bit. They're talking about the ratio (frequency) of reinforcing a kid's positive behavior versus correcting a negative behavior. I'm not sure about the science behind this idea or whether there really is an ideal ratio, but in general the point is to try to get in the habit of reinforcing a kid more often than you correct or criticize them. Most strong-willed and oppositional kids get corrected so very often that the ratio of that to reinforcement is way off, maybe 10 corrections for every one reinforcement (if that). It might be a challenge to change that ratio but well worth the effort.

You can think of it as a relational bank account. Every time you tell a kid to stop doing something or criticize them for doing it, think of it as a withdrawal from a bank account. A healthy bank account can withstand a few withdrawals. However, for an account that is mostly empty, even a small withdrawal is going to be felt much more severely. Every time you reinforce a kid, or spend time with them, draw them out in conversation, be warm and kind to them, be playful and make them laugh, you're making an emotional deposit into the account. However, each time you raise your voice, speak in an unkind way, criticize them harshly, or punish them, you're in danger of overdrawing that account. I see this often with highly authoritarian parents; the poor kid is just beaten down.

Here's the truth of it. As parents, our radar for when kids misbehave is exquisitely developed. When a kid does something that we don't like them doing, *we never miss it.* That's because we don't like the behavior. It annoys us or gets under our skin, and so our first impulse is to try to correct it as soon as possible: *I told you to stop doing that.*

However, our radar for when kids get it right isn't so nearly as well developed, i.e., we tend not to see the positive behavior and not comment on it. I'm not really sure why this is. I think it's because we feel the kid should have done the right thing in the first place so why say something? However, that's a missed opportunity for reinforcement. If you have a strong-willed child or teen who's always in trouble and has decided long ago that they're a bad kid, one of the best ways to flip that script, change that story so to speak, is to point out to them each of those times in which they got it right. I'm not advocating here for simple, hollow praise like "good job"; there is a structure and a format for doing this in a more powerful way that I'll get to in a minute.

This is a really important concept for parents to understand. Not just a parent of an oppositional and defiant kid, but the parent of any kid really. *What you think of your child is what matters the most to them.* Your attention and the positive regard you have for them, what you think of your child as a person and their positive qualities as a human being, that's what really matters to them. When kids decide that their parents don't like them (a common belief among the kids I work with), it's so terribly painful and devastating, and this belief alone can fuel the very behavior parents dislike.

I'm a great believer that most of the typical reinforcers that we hear about for kids (stickers, stamps, contracts, more computer or gaming time, etc.) are unnecessary and probably not great reinforcers anyway. There's a far more powerful way to reinforce a kid's behavior. You can use it on kids of all ages, anytime, anywhere, and it doesn't cost you a dime.

The Nurtured Heart Approach

Developed by Howard Glasser, Nurtured Heart is a great, easy-to-use way to reinforce kids on the fly. I teach it to all of the parents I work with and I highly recommend that you delve into the many resources available by Glasser to acquaint yourself with his work.

So, what is it? It's something you say to kids, and you say it in response to something they did or said that you really like and hope they do again. It's a warm, genuine way to call kids out for positive behavior and, as the name implies, what you say comes from the heart. Nurtured Heart is not to be confused with praise. Praise is just a quick, almost throwaway comment that doesn't tend to have much power or emotion behind it, such as "Thanks for putting your plate in the sink." As a reinforcer, simple praise doesn't have much juice at all and drifts away on the breeze quickly.

Nurtured Heart relentlessly energizes the positive in kids. It has three basic steps, as follows:

First, you have to stay awake and pay attention. This seems like a really simple thing but it's not. I said earlier that our radar for seeing misbehavior is excellent, but Glasser says we have this backwards. He argues that our radar for noticing the good stuff, i.e., when kids get it right, should be just as good or even better. We have to look for opportunities to reinforce and make full use of those opportunities. It can be hard for parents to make this shift and get good at it, but you'll get better with practice.

Step 2 tends to be easiest for parents in my experience. Once you notice some type of positive behavior, or the absence of a negative behavior (like ignoring a sibling who's clearly trying to provoke them rather than getting mad and provoking back), the parent just describes what they saw. Just a simple description of it, such as "I noticed when you saw the trash was full, you emptied it without being asked" or "Hey you got started on your homework right away today and got it out of the way really fast." and got it out of the way really fast."

Step 3 is a bit more challenging but it's the part that gives Nurtured Heart punch. Once you've noticed some kind of positive behavior and you have said something out loud to the kid about it, you try to include some sort of an adjective that highlights why the behavior matters (it's value) and what it says about the kid's character. For example, for the kid who empties the trash, it says they're thoughtful or helpful. For the kid who got started right away on their homework, that says they're hard working or super responsible when it comes to school. That's the cool thing about Nurtured Heart—you're not making anything up, what you say is based on the kid's own behavior that you just saw right in front of you. It's the truth of the moment. That you took time to see what they did, say something about it, and point out what that behavior says about them as a person is often very meaningful, especially for kids who get in trouble a lot.

There are a million value adjectives: kind, thoughtful, helpful, generous, loyal, loving, hardworking, giving, compassionate, gentle, intelligent, clever, playful, sweet—the list goes on and on. As parents, these are the values that we are trying to instill in our children. We want them to be kind, thoughtful and helpful human beings, both now and for the rest of their lives. Strong-willed kids get hammered so often and told everything they're doing is wrong because we frequently don't see the great stuff that's going on right in front of us.

I was sitting in an airport once waiting for my flight, and as I waited a family passed in front of me. It was a mom and dad, pushing a stroller with a girl inside who looked about a year old. Walking alongside the stroller was a boy who I guessed to be about four years old. The girl in the stroller was playing with some kind of toy that she dropped on the ground. The boy, without even thinking about it, bent over and gave the toy back to his sister. A normal, everyday kind of thing, right? It was definitely an opportunity for reinforcement. The mom or dad might have just said a simple thank you to the boy, which is what I think most of us would have done. However, that doesn't have much energy or enthusiasm behind it, although certainly it would have been better than not saying anything at all.

Remember, according to Nurtured Heart, what you think about a kid's character, and how you convey that to them is so much more powerful than just a thank you. There, right in front of you, unprompted, unscripted, is something the kid just did that represents a value within them that you want to highlight and energize.

Instead of just a simple thank you, the mom, in a very animated voice, said "Oh my goodness, look at you!" (A great way to start because what kid wouldn't turn around to see what his mom is about to say?) "Your sister dropped her toy and you picked it up for her. *What a great big brother you are!*" The mom could have chosen all kinds of other value adjectives because this one simple behavior is indicative of many positive qualities, such as being loving, kind, thoughtful, helpful, etc. However, I absolutely love *what a good big brother you are*. If he hears this said to him, over and over during his life, based just on his own behavior (no spinning it), he's going to internalize that positive image of himself as a good big brother.

Years later, when that boy is a senior in high school and his sister is a freshman, if someone messes with that girl, this boy is going to immediately come to her aid. Why? Because he's a good big brother.

What you think of your kids, and what you reflect back to them based on their own behavior that you see happening right in front of you, is the most powerful reinforcer that exists.

Don't ever underestimate the power of you.

Chief takeaways from Chapter 6

- Positive reinforcement often takes center stage in gentle parenting, and research has shown it is a powerful way to improve your child's behavior.
- However, many families with an oppositional child or teen often have trouble finding behavior to positively reinforce due to how often the kid engages in challenging behavior.
- Families often get into a mutual cycle of negativity, leaving little room for noticing the positive behavior that is likely occurring every day.
- This creates emotional distance, and this disconnection often fuels the very behavior in kids that we don't care for.
- It is helpful for you to get into the habit of noticing positive behavior more often, which is likely present at least some of the time and try to reinforce it more often than you correct.
- Parents are the most powerful reinforcers that exist The Nurtured Heart Approach, developed by Howard Glasser, provides a structured way to relentlessly notice, comment on, and energize your child's positive behavior and the values that behavior represents.

Pause, Earn, and Return 7

A Better Alternative than Punishment

Now it's time to turn our attention to some really cool interventions and strategies that are highly effective with even the most challenging, oppositional and defiant kids. As I mentioned earlier in the book, these are interventions that I've taught hundreds of parents so they're well vetted and battle tested. While no intervention works every single time, I think by and large you're going to find these to be very useful to reduce conflict with your child or teen and help them respond to you in far more positive way.

Pause, Earn, and Return Reinforcement (Negative Reinforcement)

I briefly touched on the idea of negative reinforcement in Chapter 3, but I want to expand on it here. Negative reinforcement is the underlying principle behind just about every consequence I recommend to families, and it's essential that you understand what it is so that you can apply it effectively in your own family. I want to first distinguish negative reinforcement from punishment because they're really not the same thing at all.

Punishment

People often use the word "consequence" when really what they're referring to is punishment. The word consequence is actually really more of a generic term, but to a psychologist, punishment means something very specific.

From strictly a behavioral perspective, punishment is when a child does something they're not supposed to do, or doesn't do something

DOI: 10.4324/9781003452638-10

they should have done, and the parent then imposes a fixed penalty of some kind. Something happens that the kid doesn't like after they behave in a negative way. The essential feature of a punishment is that once the penalty is given, there's really no opportunity to undo it. For example, if I speed on the freeway and get pulled over, the officer is going to give me a ticket, and there's nothing I can do about that no matter how well I drive from that moment forward. It's done and I can't undo it. That's how our justice system works—if you do the crime, you do the time.

There are many examples of how punishment is used with kids, such as:

For younger kids:
Being sent to bed early for not listening.
Losing dessert for not behaving during dinner.
Having a toy taken away for a week for hitting a sibling.
Having a tablet taken away for a day for throwing a tantrum.

For teenagers:
Losing their phone for a few weeks because they failed a class.
Not being allowed to see friends on the weekend for getting detention.
Having their gaming system locked up for 24 hours for cursing.
Being grounded for a month for smoking marijuana.

You can see that what each of these has in common is that the penalty is fixed and there's nothing the kid can do about it other than serving out their time. There are numerous problems with punishment.

First, I've never found that punishment works all that well with kids. It just doesn't seem to produce any kind of lasting behavior change in my opinion. Kids might work to avoid the punishment, but I don't think it does much to convince them that whatever they did wasn't okay.

Second, often when you give a kid a punishment, they just get mad the minute you give it. They obviously broke a rule of some kind and might have been really upset when they broke it, but if you drop a punishment on them, now they're just going to get mad all over again and you will have to deal with that. One problem (breaking the rule) has now turned into two problems (getting mad about the punishment). Since the penalty can't be undone, many kids at that point figure they've got nothing to lose so they might as well let loose on their parents and so many do. Furthermore, parents often, out of frustration, drop the punishment right as the negative behavior is occurring, which only serves to further inflame the kid. (That's a very bad idea; far better to wait until the kid has calmed down before delivering a consequence.)

Third, once the penalty has been imposed, such as a kid losing their phone for a week, you've lost the phone as a source of leverage for that entire week. You can't take a phone away twice, so that tool is no longer available to you for a solid week. Yes, I know you could extend the time of the restriction, but I don't think that works well. The kid just gets angry again and the phone's return just moves even farther and farther out of reach. Or, worse still, some parents just keep adding more days of restriction in the heat of the moment. If you're not sure what this looks like, watch the movie *The Breakfast Club* and scene in the library when the teacher keeps adding weekend detentions. It's totally ineffective as it makes the adult look foolish and the kid almost heroic.

Therefore, for all of these reasons, I recommend that parents use punishment very rarely. In just about every instance, for almost any problem behavior you're wanting to change, there is a far more effective alternative.

Negative Reinforcement

As said earlier in the book, negative reinforcement is a bit confusing so bear with me on this. The term was coined by the late behavioral psychologist B.F. Skinner, and it's a terrible name because it really doesn't tell you what it is and it's hard to remember. I've thought long and hard on coming up with a better, more descriptive name. Nothing came to me so naturally I asked someone smarter than myself and here's what ChatGPTcame up with: *Pause, Earn, and Return Reinforcement*. That's not bad, actually.

Here's the basic idea. When a kid does something that isn't okay or doesn't do something that you wanted them to do, you temporarily withhold some type of high-interest privilege until the desired behavior occurs. So, you put a pause on the privilege (the reinforcer) and don't return it until the kid does what they're supposed to do.

This offers a number of advantages over punishment. First, it often avoids that second problem, i.e., the kid getting mad when they receive the consequence. It incentives them to accept the consequence because starting right at that moment they can begin to earn back the privilege. Second, it also incentives the kid to engage in positive behavior (and refrain from the negative behavior) because that's the only way to earn back what was lost.

Here are some examples that include the negative behavior in question and what you would say to the kid:

For younger kids:

Behavior:	What you'd say:
Whining	"Happy to give you what you want when you're using a big kid voice."
Tantrum	"Happy to talk once you're calm."
Fighting with a sibling	"The only way you can get some time on your tablet today is by being nice to your brother for a while" (as opposed to punishment, which would be "You lost your tablet for fighting with you brother.")
Stalling at bedtime	"Call me once you're in bed and I'll come read you a story" (as opposed to "You lost story time because you're late getting into bed.")

For a teenager:

Behavior:	What you'd say:
Being disrespectful	"I'd like you to put your phone up on the counter until you can be respectful to me for a while" (as opposed to "You've lost your phone for a week for being disrespectful.")
Not starting homework	"No using the Xbox today until you finish those missing assignments."
Cursing at you	"If you expect to see your friends this weekend then I suggest you speak to me in a different way" (as opposed to "You can't see your friends this weekend because you cursed at me.")
Not waking up to an alarm	"You're welcome to take your phone to school any day that you're up to your alarm."

You probably get the idea. "You no longer get this until you do that." *Pause, earn, and return* … The kid can only earn the privilege back once they've given you the positive behavior in question (which is really just the absence of the negative behavior).

You'll notice too that in these examples I said that the child or teen needs to engage in the positive behavior "for a while" without specifying how long that actually is. I think it works best when you do not tell a kid how long it will be before the privilege is reinstated. There are a couple of reasons for this.

First, you simply don't know how long that will be because it depends on several factors, starting with how well they accepted the consequence. If you didn't get a lot of pushback when the consequence is given (the kid doesn't argue with you about it or get super angry), you'd probably want to return the privilege a lot faster. By returning the privilege sooner, you are reinforcing the acceptance of the consequence, which is worth a lot to you. Remember how I said that with punishment your child often gets really angry when the penalty is given? That's the cool thing about pause, earn, and return. Kids push back a lot less because they know that they have the opportunity for the privilege to be reinstated sooner if they don't make a fuss. If I say, "Please put your phone up on the counter until you can be respectful to me for a while," the kid is now massively incentivized to put the phone on the counter without an upset because "a while" doesn't begin until they do so.

Second, you'll probably want to consider how serious the negative behavior in question is before deciding on the length of the pause. In general, the more serious the behavior, the longer the pause. For example, if the kid spent 20 minutes yelling and cursing at you, that's going to be a much longer pause than a few minutes of mild disrespect. Furthermore, you never know what the kid might do during the pause that might get you to reconsider its length.

For example, if they lost a privilege for being mean to a sibling but then they were over-the-top super sweet to them for a bit, or even funny how they went about it, you would make the pause shorter. However, if the kid lost their phone for hitting their sibling, the pause will be longer because hitting someone is a big deal. That behavior should be parked in a different bucket relative to, say, some bickering between siblings. I might also play with the length of the pause if there's a pattern of the same behavior and I've already tried a shorter pause without success.

A quick word on the length of time a kid might lose a privilege. I've found that parents are often tempted to make the length of a consequence too long. It is not at all uncommon at the start of treatment for a parent to tell me that their kid lost their phone for an entire summer. While there is some correlation between the length of a consequence and its potency (effectiveness), it's only a very weak correlation. The consequence can be so long that the kid gives up all hope of the privilege being returned. This can lead to what adolescent therapist Russell Rice calls the "Dead Man Walking" syndrome: if a kid has no hope, they might as well follow their anger and get more out of it. Without hope, they also experience more anger and may want to get retribution and punish their parents by making them equally miserable. Focusing on earn and return reduces this likelihood. This whole point is not to make kids suffer, but to get them back on track.

I've found that in most cases, pausing something briefly (e.g., an hour, a day, or at most a couple of days), works just fine, and anything over that you quickly reach a point of diminishing returns. Remember too that when you reinstate a privilege, it's now yours to pause again whenever you need to. For every teenager I know, losing their phone for even an hour is *the worst thing ever*.

Here's a heads up on this "for a while" thing. Your kid is going to hate it at first. They'll insist that you must tell them how long they've lost the privilege for, how unfair it is that you won't, how they can't possibly start the consequence until you tell them how long, and so on. I think not telling a kid a set amount of time makes them feel off balance and not in control. In a way, however, this is consistent with the larger message you're trying to send: *These are the rules in our family. You don't have agree with them, but you still need to follow them.*

Kids will get used to this "for a while" thing eventually, but when you start trying it out expect resistance. I recommended you just say, "I can't tell you how long because truthfully I don't know how long. In part, that depends on how well you accept the consequence. You can start right now if you like and get your phone back sooner. Or maybe you'd rather start tomorrow. I don't know, I'll let you decide on that. But, I'm not giving you your phone back until you've been respectful for a while." It's paradoxical to say "You can start that tomorrow if you like," but oddly it often works with kids. It's probably because that's a roundabout way of telling them that behaving in a way that works against their own self-interests doesn't make any sense, and that time is on your side and not theirs (they have to comply eventually in order to get the privilege reinstated).

Here is an example of negative reinforcement from my own life.

When our youngest was around 12 years old, my wife and I decided we'd take her out to get ice cream. What's better, right? The problem is our daughter was in a pre-teen mood that day and once we got into the car, she was just a perpetual grump. We tried to cajole her out of it but no luck and she was still irritable, so I said, "Hmm. Okay as now I'm thinking ice cream is off the table so let's just go run some errands." Predictably, she asked why no ice cream. My response was (in a very matter-of-fact, not at all irritable tone):

> "Because you've been a grump. I'm just not in an ice cream getting mood anymore. But, I'll tell you what. You could easily put me back in an ice cream mood and I'll give you few options on how to do that. Option 1 is you could sing us a song. Not just any old song, not something that nobody likes, like the happy birthday song. A real song. Option 2, you could tell us a joke. No knock-knock jokes, but an actual funny joke. And, last, Option 3, is you could be nice to us for a while. Any of those will do."

I turned around and my wife and I started talking as if she wasn't even behind us. As I've mentioned earlier in the book, we wanted to set the tone in the car and just because our daughter was vibrating it didn't mean we were going to vibrate along with her. Five minutes later, she pokes her head between our seats, smiles, and says, "Hi guys!"

This is most definitely negative reinforcement (pause, earn, and return) and it worked really well. I think too because I was playful with her and a little absurd (not disrespectful, just goofy), it worked even better. However, what if I had used punishment instead and just told her that she'd lost ice cream because of how she was talking to us? Her response would have been 100% predictable: She would just gotten mad and probably would have stayed mad at us the rest of the day. I can't see how that would have been a useful intervention in any way or a teaching opportunity either. Instead, here's the message we did send to her: people don't want to spend time with a grump, but sometimes you can still switch it up and still win them over.

As I mentioned, it's not that punishment is never the way to go. I'm just advocating that you use it rarely, and instead use pause, earn, and return as often as you can. On occasion, you can use a blend of negative reinforcement and punishment when negative reinforcement can't be used or it's impractical to use it. Our justice system does that—10 years in prison for burglary (punishment) but time off for good behavior (negative reinforcement).

For example, let's say your teenager has an 11:00 p.m. curfew but keeps coming home late. Not the crime of the century obviously, but you really don't want them out that late. I, for sure, would not give them a consequence the first or even the second time it happened (assuming it's not 4:00 in the morning when they arrive home), but I definitely would give a consequence the third time. A blend of punishment and negative reinforcement would be, "Since you've been late coming home a couple of times, I'm going to drop your curfew down to 10:00 pm for a while. Be on time for a while and we can go back to 11:00 again. However, if you can't stick to 10:00, then I'm probably not going to let you go out for a couple of weekends and then we can try again."

I promise you negative reinforcement works far better than punishment. Throughout the rest of this book, I'm going to give you many practical examples of how to use it to address all kinds of challenging behaviors.

Chief takeaways from Chapter 7

- We often use the word "consequences" but what people really mean by that most of the time is punishment. A punishment is a penalty of some kind for negative behavior that lasts for a fixed amount of time ("You've lost your phone for a week").
- Punishment doesn't work very well. It doesn't teach kids very much and it usually just makes them mad.
- However, strong-willed and oppositional kids do need to be held accountable, especially if the same negative behavior occurs over and over. Kids don't have to agree with the rules, but they need to follow them anyway.
- There's a far better alternative to punishment but it has a really confusing name: negative reinforcement. A better name for it is might be pause, earn, and return reinforcement.
- That's when a privilege of some kind is paused or held back until the child or teen engages in the desired positive behavior for an unspecified period of time. "Please put your phone up on the counter and I'll give it back once you've been respectful to me for a while."
- It's best not to give a time frame for the privilege to be returned, but in general, shorter consequences are often just as effective as longer ones.

A Framework for Much Better Behavior

8

In this chapter, we're going to pivot a bit and start to focus on strategies and interventions to address negative behavior and incentivize much more positive behavior. Thus far, we've focused on how to stay matter-of-fact, set reasonable limits, have high expectations, disengage, not argue, sidestep red herrings, and use pause, earn, and return reinforcement. From this point forward, we'll be getting more into the weeds of how to vastly improve your child or teen's behavior. Remember, the use of positive reinforcement is also essential but it's probably not going to be sufficient all by itself to bring about the kinds of changes you're wanting in your family.

Again, as I discussed earlier in the book, your child or teen doesn't like behaving in negative ways. They might give the appearance of liking or enjoying it, but I promise you they don't and they want you to set limits with them. Once you get into a rhythm of not allowing negative behavior and responding to it differently, your kid is going to feel much better about themselves and you're going to feel much closer to them.

Here's another truism that I've learned about kids: they feel better when they do better, not the other way around. Most people (including many therapists) believe that you have to help a child or teen feel better (for example, less angry or depressed) first in order for them to behave in a different way at home or at school. In my years of doing this work, I just don't think this is true. Instead, once parents are able to significantly improve their child's behavior (once they do better), kids then start to feel better, i.e., they look, sound, and describe themselves as much happier.

Remember too that it's important that you hold your kids to very high standards behaviorally, and relentlessly convey to them a sense of optimism and certainty that they can meet those expectations. Always assume that your kids want to do better (because they really do), but they just don't know how to do better without your help and support.

DOI: 10.4324/9781003452638-11

Leveraging Incentives

Often in my sessions with parents, they will describe many behaviors that their kid engages in that they understandably don't care for, such as: not following directions; yelling; cursing; having temper tantrums (more commonly referred to as emotional dysregulation with teens); low motivation; falling behind on homework; damaging property; physical aggression; and so on. I've worked with many particularly difficult kids who might engage in all of those behaviors rather than a combination of them, and maybe your child or teen does as well. A child's emotions that tend to go hand in hand with these behaviors are anger, depression, and anxiety. Therefore, if you want to help a child experience these emotions less often and more often experience joy, love, contentment, pride, and satisfaction, you have to begin by improving their behavior. Again, kids feel better when they do better.

Here's one of the secrets to changing behavior for the better: you have to give your child or teen a reason not to engage in negative behavior. We're going to need to engineer your home environment in such a way as to disincentivize your child or teen's negative behavior. Simply telling them often over and over to be respectful, do their homework, not to overreact to being told no, that alone will do nothing to change their behavior for the better. If it did, you wouldn't be reading this book.

So, what's in it for your child or teen currently to behave in ways that aren't okay? It probably seems like a mystery to you. What possible reason could they have for being so oppositional or disrespectful, particularly when you've not raised them to be that way or they have siblings that don't do those things?

In most cases, there are quite a few hidden incentives that drive and maintain negative behavior over time. As I mentioned previously, in the case of a temper tantrum or emotional upset, the incentive for that behavior is that it gets and holds your attention. I've also talked about the importance of disengaging, i.e., walking away from your kid if they start to become angry and disrespectful, but while important, disengaging alone won't stop kids from getting really angry and doing things that aren't okay. You must give them a reason, i.e., one or more incentives, which typically will be things that they can earn or access only on days in which they've met your behavioral expectations.

In most cases, the negative behavior in question serves a hidden function—it does something for the kid that benefits them in some way. Here's a list of behaviors and the likely function those behaviors serve:

Behavior	Function(s)
Tantrums or dysregulation	Holding parents' attention; task avoidance; not being held accountable; hoping a "no" will turn into a "yes"
Not following directions	Not having to do something they don't want to do
Disrespect	Shutting down conversations that kids don't care to have; not being held accountable; gaining power and control over their environment
Not doing homework or chores	Avoiding difficult or unpleasant tasks
Physical aggression	Intimidating others to gain control; obtaining the ability to blame others and avoid taking personal responsibility ("She made me mad, so I hit her")
Following you around the house terrorizing	If you're going to make me unhappy, I will make you unhappy.
Not waking up to an alarm	Getting extra sleep; convincing parents that they are incapable ("I can't help it I just sleep through my alarm") so they take on the responsibility of keeping the kid moving in the morning rather than doing it themselves
Refusing to get a driver's license	Temporarily reducing the anxiety of learning how to drive through avoidance; avoiding the effort it takes to get a license; ensuring that someone else will do the driving

Even some of the more serious behaviors I see in my practice serve a clear but often overlooked function. For example, teenagers will self-harm for many reasons, but most often the function of that behavior serves to influence the behavior of someone else, such as eliciting caretaking from parents or peers; task avoidance ("I can't go to school because I'll get overwhelmed and hurt myself"); or expressing anger when they feel wronged so that someone else will feel bad ("Look what you made me do"). I know that kids will often say they hurt themselves because it makes them feel better and in some cases that's true, but far less often than we might think.

Since the onset of COVID, more kids are now reporting an increase in school-related anxiety, sometimes to the point where they stop going to school altogether. Parents and schools respond in a supportive way by putting the kid on a less demanding schedule or type of independent study program at home. I can see the logic in this, but often this approach backfires because it can incentivize kids to report even more anxiety. If reporting anxiety results in a reduction of demands relative to school (doing homework, getting up early, sitting through classes, etc.), then kids are incentivized to report even more anxiety. Additionally, lowering expectations around school can also incentivize a child or teen not to benefit from whatever therapy they might be receiving for this if the underlying function of the anxiety is to avoid the demands of school.

Please know that I am in no way judging kids for any of this. There's something called the principle of least effort—the tendency for people to find the least effortful solution to a problem or task. This is just how human beings work—we all respond to incentives. If you give someone an incentive for doing something, there's a good chance they're going to keep doing it even if the reinforcement takes place outside of their conscious awareness. What gets reinforced, gets repeated.

This same principle applies for oppositional and defiant kids. You have to give them a reason, i.e., an incentive, to change their behavior or their behavior very likely isn't going to change.

The first step is to identify what your child or teen really wants and leverage that for better behavior. The actual incentives you'll use will depend a bit on your child's age. The list for younger kids might include: watching TV; playing outside; going on a fun outing on the weekend; having play dates with friends; sleepovers; a later bedtime; and time on a tablet. The list is shorter for older kids and teenagers but the items on the list have much more power or juice: access to their phones (the number one incentive for teens); time on gaming systems (this has the same juice but not all kids game); and face-to-face time with friends, either after school on the weekends. Your own child might have other incentives or privileges that they'll work for, but these seem to be the big ones in my experience.

Daily Leveraging

In my experience, it is highly effective for parents to have a list of daily privileges (incentives) that a kid can earn each day based on the absence of key negative behaviors, which in turn increases the frequency of neutral or positive behaviors (positive reinforcement).

"Each day" here is the key. Often, a parent might say "you can earn x for going a week doing y." I just don't think that works very well. Some kids act out so often, or they've been in the habit of doing things for so long that aren't okay, that asking to "be good" for a week in order to earn a reward feels an eternity for them. Instead, if you give your child or teen access to something that they really want to do each day, then every day becomes a fresh restart, a do-over of sorts if the incentive wasn't earned the day prior.

For example, let's say a kid really wants and values time on a tablet or gaming system and you've decided to use that as your primary daily incentive (a wise choice). I've learned that the best way to structure this is not to allow the kid to use the device until as late in the day as possible after they've earned it by meeting your expectations (engaging in whatever positive behaviors you've established). This is important because you want the incentive in place all day to keep your child's motivation high throughout the day. If you give the kid access to the incentive too early in the day, you've weakened their motivation to behave in a positive way for the remainder of the day.

In order to get access to a privilege, often a screen of some sort, the child or teen must have met your expectations that day. For example, for a younger child who tantrums, the expectation would be that they need to be tantrum-free to have time on their device later in the day. If the kid does have a tantrum that day and does not earn the device time that evening, they begin earning it all over again the next day. This is a blend of traditional positive reinforcement along with an element of pause and return reinforcement.

I'm going to give you many examples of how to use this approach to change just about any behavior, including getting kids to be more respectful, clean their rooms, help out around the house, do homework, get a part-time job, a driver's license, and so on.

Here's something crucial to remember about situations in which a child or teen ends up not earning an incentive at the end of a day. Let's go back to the kid who has temper tantrums and to earn some tablet time in the evening the expectation is that it must be a tantrum-free day. At first, the child will still lose their temper over something and get really upset, thereby not earning time on the tablet later that day. It is really important that you not tell the kid they didn't earn their tablet time, especially right in the middle of the tantrum as this will almost certainly make the tantrum worse. I'm telling you this because sometimes parents have a strong temptation to deliver the consequence right as the negative behavior is occurring, but I promise you it's best to resist this urge as it'll be like throwing gas on a fire.

A better alternative is to say nothing about the tablet and wait for the kid to ask you about it. Sometimes, they know they've lost it and it's okay to just confirm that. If they start to get worked up again, you can say, "I know that's disappointing. But now you're working on earning it tomorrow, assuming things go well between now and then." Often kids are smarter than to ask right away if it's obvious they've already lost the incentive, hoping, I suspect, that by some miracle you'll forget and still give them time on the tablet that evening.

Here's another important point: kids should never have access to their daily incentive without asking you for it first. In that case, since they need permission to get on the tablet, again say nothing during or right after the tantrum and wait for them to ask about it later in the day. The conversation might flow like this:

CHILD (C):   Can I get on my tablet please?

PARENT (P):   How am I going to do THAT? *[Note: I love wording it this way. I learned it from former FBI hostage negotiator Chris Voss, the author of* Never Split the Difference: Negotiating as If Your Life Depended on It. *Kids generally are never quite sure how to respond and it'll cause them to stop and think for a second.]*

(C):   Uh, I don't know. You can just let me have it.

(P):   I suppose I could, but what's the problem with that?

(C):   I don't know, there's no problem.

(P):   No? What happened earlier today?

(C):   I don't remember.

(P):   Okay, well take some time to think on it and we can talk when you're ready. *[Note: I think it's vital that kids not avoid talking about their negative behavior. In this conversation, I'm wanting them to take some accountability for what happened, which includes having a brief, respectful, not angry conversation about it. I know they really want the tablet so when I say "take some time to think about it" that incentivizes them to stick with the conversation. If, instead, they walk* *away, it's a certainty that they'll come back again (sometimes right away, sometimes later but rarely much later) and be willing to talk about it because they know it's the only way you will give them access to the device again. When this happens, just pick up right where you left off. In addition to talking about the negative behavior, I want them to do so in a respectful, non-defensive way, so feel free to end the conversation as many times as you need to in order for this to happen. It's easiest and most effective to talk through problems or issues right before the kid is expecting their incentive to be returned because that's when their motivation is the highest.]*

(C): Okay, I got mad when you told me to clean up my room.

(P): That's true. And what did you do when you were mad?

(C): I yelled at you. Threw things at you.

(P): And you know that's not okay, right? I mean, it's okay to be mad, sure, everyone gets mad, but it's never okay to yell at me and throw things, no matter how mad you are. We don't do that in our family.

(C): I know it wasn't okay, I'm sorry. *[NOTE: If, instead of apologizing, the kid blames you or someone else for getting mad, gets mean to you, tries to justify what they did, end the conversation by saying: "That's not what I'm wanting from this conversation. No blaming or talking to me in a mean way please. I'm going to end the conversation, but you're welcome to come back to me anytime you're ready to talk to me about this is a better way, and then we can talk about your tablet." Again, don't be afraid to end the conversation as many times as you have to for your child or teen to pull off the conversation in a reasonable way.]*

(P): I appreciate you apologizing. So, no on the tablet today as I think you already know but I'd be happy to give you time on it tomorrow assuming things go well the rest of tonight and tomorrow, of course. Thanks for talking this through with me, I appreciate that.

The Premack Principle

David Premack, an experimental psychologist, came up with a very simple concept that is highly useful with strong-willed and oppositional kids.

The application of the Premack principle consists of asking that they do a less preferred task before giving them permission to do a more preferred task. For example, you might ask that your younger child to clean up their room before going outside to play or go see a friend, or a teenager to do their homework before gaming or spending time on their phones.

This works really well with kids, and it helps to create a sort of "standard operating procedure" in your family that's ideally established when your kids are still young (but it can be established at any time really). It's kind of a work-before-fun way of looking at things. This is a great value to instill in your kids, i.e., that responsibilities come before fun or recreation. I don't think human beings are naturally wired that way, we tend to want to play first and take care of business second. It's a value that we must learn over time, but once instilled, it benefits kids greatly as they move into adulthood.

I don't see parents capitalize on this nearly as often as they should. It's pretty common for the kids I treat to have all kinds of uncompleted tasks (chores not done, a messy room, lots of homework, etc.) but they're still spending tons of time on their phones or gaming systems, or out seeing their friends. Capitalize on those moments when kids really want to do something—that's when they're most highly motivated to do something they really don't want to do and give you the least amount of grief when you ask them to do it.

Also, if you have a kid who just isn't great at following through on tasks or responsibilities, it's best never to agree to the "deal" I often see kids offer to their parents, "If you let me see my friends tonight, I promise I'll do my homework tomorrow." If your kid is super responsible then of course you can agree to that sometimes, but far more often parents are left holding the bag and the homework never gets done.

Work before fun, that's the rule.

Stopping Negative Behavior as It's Unfolding: Using an If/Then Statement

In addition to leveraging incentives, making use of if/then statements can be highly effective.

The idea here is that sometimes it can be really helpful to give kids a reminder of what incentive they're hoping to earn (or not lose) when they begin to behave in a negative way. An if/then statement tends to work the best if you make it early on as the negative behavior is just starting to present itself. If a kid is already escalated and angry, you can still make an if/then statement but it's less powerful and less likely to be effective.

If/then is exactly as it sounds: if this, then that. The "this" is usually the incentive that the kid is hoping to earn or not lose, and the "that" is the behavior in question, which is starting to unfold that you're hoping to stop.

Here are some examples of if/then statements (as always, to be made by you in a matter-of-fact, neutral way):

- "If you expect to be on your phone later today, then I suggest I'm going to need you to be more respectful between now and then."
- "You've asked to go to a sleepover this weekend. If you'd like to go, then I'd like your room cleaned up first please for me to say yes to that."
- "If you want time on your tablet tonight here's what needs to happen first, please."
- "We had talked about going to see a movie today, but I can't see that happening if you don't start treating your brother in a better way."
- "I know you're hoping for some time to game later today. I'm not sure how that's going to happen if you don't go to your room to cool off in the way as I asked you to."
- "If you expect to take your phone to school with you, then I'm going to need you to be up to your alarm and ready to walk out the door on time."

There are all kinds of ways you can vary if/then statements, but the meaning is still the same: dial back whatever you're doing that's not okay or do the thing that still needs to be done, otherwise you're not going to get the fun thing you're wanting to do.

There is an interesting quirk about if/then statements that you should know. When you make an if/then statement, it almost never works (stops the negative behavior) right away. You'll say it and for a while the kid will continue to do whatever they were doing, so don't expect them to immediately stop the negative behavior. I think what happens is that it takes a few minutes for them to think what you just said through, to penetrate the fog so to speak. I also think that there's an element of the kid not wanting to lose face and that would happen if they acquiesced right away. Instead, in my experience, you'll likely see your child or teen sputter out: "What? I don't care about my phone anyway. Go ahead and take... you can't do that... it's not fair... I can't believe you'd... ahhh!"

Usually, the sputtering occurs as they're walking away from you. Here again, resist the temptation to say anything, just stop talking, turn your back and walk away, and then let the if/then statement do its job for you. And, of course, if the child continues on a negative path, you'll always want to deliver the consequence and be super consistent about that. If you only sometimes give your kid a consequence when they've truly earned it, then they'll not take you seriously and it'll take that much longer for you to improve their behavior (if you ever improve it at all).

Room Time

I've never really understood why some of the gentle parenting books say not to give kids time-outs or send them to their bedrooms. I find that very odd because I've found that sending kids to their rooms for a short while works great but only if you set it up in a very particular way as follows.

Here's the rationale for sending kids to their rooms for brief time-outs (for teenagers, it's better and more age-appropriate to refer to it as time in their rooms rather than a time-out). If a kid is mad at you, it's very difficult for them to cool off while still in your presence. That's one of the reasons why I recommend disengaging from angry and disrespectful kids because it also creates physical space between you and them. As I've said, everyone calms down eventually, that's a certainty, but physical space usually increases the speed at which this happens. Additionally, when kids are away from you, or you're away from them, so you can't "ping" off each other, i.e., exchange less-than-helpful comments with each other.

Most parents abandon the use of time-out or room time because kids will often put up a big fight and refuse to go. It makes sense—why would they go to their rooms when told to? They already weren't following directions, so how can you expect them to follow one more direction to go to their rooms? Wouldn't it be great though if they did? If you could easily get them to their rooms, you could quickly and peacefully disrupt any kind of emerging negative behavior, get the kid away from whoever is bugging them (maybe that's you), give them the time and space to calm down, and then emerge from their rooms in a much better frame of mind.

As is true of any behavior, to get your kid to go to their room when asked, you have to give them a good reason to do so.

First, there's no reason to send kids to their rooms for an eternity. Just a few minutes of being in their room is generally just as effective as longer periods, unless the kid is unusually worked up. Here's the incentive: if your child or teen goes to their room when asked, without carrying on about it, arguing, and so on, then you'll only ask them to stay there for a few minutes. As an aside, that piece of advice you might have heard about one minute of time-out for every year of the child's age? I think that's made up. For kids of just about any age, a short time-out works just fine. Remember, it's not a punishment, it's a reset and that often takes hardly any time at all.

However, if a kid doesn't go when asked, makes a big deal about it, yells and what have you, then the time-out or room time is longer, maybe 10 minutes at most. A short time-out, therefore, if they go peacefully, a longer time-out if they don't.

Note that you can't just spring this short versus long thing on kids, you'll need to set it up in advance, and explain what you'll be doing in this way:

> *"Hey, you know sometimes when I ask you to go to your room to cool off, sometimes you don't go right away do you? I'd really like you to please because that's a lot easier and you can get back to whatever you were doing a lot faster. How about this? If you go right away, I'll only ask to be in your room hardly anytime at all, a ridiculously short amount of time, so short you won't believe it, maybe a minute. But if you don't go right away, I'll ask you stay down there a longer, say 10 minutes."*

I think it's fun when you set this up with kids, especially younger kids, that you do it in an easy, almost playful way. What really makes it playful is you can show the kid the difference between a long and short time-out (room time) by letting your kids practice what those look like by actually giving you the time-out, which they absolutely will love doing. When a kid ends up getting a long time-out because they've refused to go or have argued about it, it's best never to say, "Now you'll be down there longer." This just makes them mad. They'll quickly come to understand what makes something a long time-out, so no need to explain it if they refuse to go.

I recommend too that you go to the kid's rooms to take them off their time-out rather than letting them just wander out whenever they feel like it. If they can talk briefly to you about why you sent them there and have that conversation in a neutral or reasonably polite way, they can come out. If not, just walk away and let them know you'll come back later (a few minutes) and try again until they can tell you in at least a neutral way why they were sent there.

It'll take a while for your kids to get into a rhythm of taking their time-outs easily, likely at least a few weeks depending on how often you give them. Note too that most kids will still get longer time-outs sometimes, that's inevitable. I find on average that for most kids about three out of four time-outs will be short ones, so you'll still see plenty of the longer ones too.

If the kid decides not to take their time-out when asked, go ahead and disengage and say just once, "Your time-out starts when you're in your room" and nothing else. You might need to outwait them, but really nothing happens until they take the time-out no matter how long it takes them to do so. For a kid who's really digging in and refusing to take their time-out, you can make an if/then statement, again just once: "If you to expect to _____, then I suggest you go to your room and get it over with." Wait out the kid as long as you need to—life for them basically stops until they're ready to take their time-out.

We're now at the point in the book where we're going to shift our focus from talking about foundational skills and begin talking about the specific interventions you can use to tackle all kinds of behavioral issues common to opposition and defiant children and teens.

Chief takeaways from Chapter 8

- Children and teenagers feel better when they do better, not the other way around. Once a kid's behavior improves and there is less conflict at home, they begin to thrive, feel better about themselves, and have closer relationships with the people who love them.

- Kids need a reason to change their behavior beyond your just asking them over and over to do so. Negative behavior often serves a hidden function, i.e., the behavior has a value to the kid that's often hard to see.

- It's essential that kids be given incentives to improve their behavior. It's best to identify positive incentives, which can be leveraged on a daily basis for better behavior. The most readily available, and typically most powerful incentive is access to screens or time with friends.

- Make full use of the simple, but totally amazing, Premack principle. Only letting your child or teen do something that they enjoy after they've met your behavioral expectations and daily responsibilities is a powerful incentive and instills a value that will carry your child far in life.

- If/then statements can be used effectively when a kid is starting to dig in on something before it turns into something bigger. For example, you might say, "If you expect to be on your phone or laptop later today, then I'm going to need you to speak to me in a nicer way please."

- Asking kids to go to their bedrooms for very short time periods can be really helpful. However, for that not to turn into a battle, you're going to need to set that up in a way you haven't thought about before (long/short).

The Mental Health Benefits of Reducing Screen Time and Using It to Incentivize Better Behavior

9

My goal for this chapter is an ambitious one: to do a deep dive into the negative effects of screen time (phones, tablets, gaming systems, and so on) and to teach you some highly effective strategies that will incentivize your child or teen to change just about any behavior in a positive way. Leveraging screens is by far the single most powerful incentive for any kid, which is why we're going to make full use of it. This is a complex topic so we're going to be covering a lot of ground, but bear with me because I promise it's worth your time and attention.

Screens present an odd paradox from a behavior change perspective. Time on devices has the potential to harm children in so many ways that I will summarize for you in this chapter. Managing screen time, making sure kids stay within and not exceed the "safe" number of hours per day on a device, and monitoring their online activity is probably the single best option you have as a parent to lower the probability that your child will develop a mental health condition, such as depression, anxiety, and self-harm/suicide. If your child or teen already has a mental health condition, getting a handle on their screen time is also a vital component to helping them get better, one that is often overlooked by both parents and therapists.

Once you feel like you understand the relationship between screen time and its contribution to childhood mental health challenges and you've taken steps to safely manage screen time in your family, we can move on to leveraging the power of devices to elicit and maintain vastly improved behavior.

DOI: 10.4324/9781003452638-12

The Relationship between Screens and Childhood Mental Health Issues

I'm going to summarize what I know about this topic, both the research on the negative effects of screens and what I've learned in my own clinical practice. If you want to learn even more and delve further into this topic, I covered this in quite a bit of detail in *Family-Focused Treatment for Child and Adolescent Mental Health: A New Paradigm.*

We are in the midst of a mental health epidemic among children and teens. Our current U.S. Surgeon General, Vivek Murthy, calls the increase in childhood mental health challenges as the "defining public health crisis of our time."

When I'm doing some kind of speaking engagement, I'll often ask the audience when they feel this epidemic began. Most commonly, people think all of this started with COVID. While it's true the pandemic made things worse, the increase in mental health challenges in young people actually predated COVID by almost a decade. For example, per CDC data, the percentage of youth reporting suicidal thoughts in 2011 was 16%, but by 2021 that had increased to 22%. The percentage of young people who have experienced persistent feelings of sadness or hopelessness increased from 28% to 42% in that same time period.

What happened around 2011? The likely culprit (or one of them anyway) was the introduction of smartphones and other devices.

In her book, *iGen: Why Today's Super-Connected Kids Are Growing Up Less Rebellious, More Tolerant, Less Happy—and Completely Unprepared for Adulthood—and What That Means for the Rest of Us,* Jean Twenge, Professor of Psychology at San Diego State University, argues very convincingly that the decline in our children's mental health started around 2010–2011 when a majority of children and teens acquired smartphones.

If I could do only one thing to reverse the current childhood mental health epidemic, it would be to help parents substantially reduce the number of hours per day their child or teen spend on a screen and more safely monitor their online activity.

Most parents who I work with seem to have a general understanding that too much time on devices isn't good for kids. When I ask them why they think that, the most common answer they give is "social media." This is partially true, but often not for the reason people think, and that as an explanation alone is incomplete. I'm going to take you through each of the contributing factors one by one, and then we'll move onto a discussion of how as a parent you can mitigate each of these negative influences, thereby buffering your child against developing a mental health problem.

Dose-Related Effect

The number of hours a child or teen spends on a device each day matters. In general, the more time each day a kid is on a screen, the greater the likelihood of developing a mental health problem, such as depression or anxiety. For example, researcher Mingli Liu and her colleagues conducted a meta-analysis (a kind of statistical analysis that combines and analyzes the results of multiple studies) and found that the risk of depression increases by 13% for each additional hour a kid spends engaged with social media.

Along these same lines, Yvonne Kelly and her colleagues at the University College London, found that for girls who spent less than three hours per day on social media, 18.1% developed depressive symptoms. However, for girls who spent more than five hours per day, that jumped to 38.1%. Kelly found that although boys were somewhat less affected by social media use, their rates of depressive symptoms also increased in a corresponding manner.

Think of it in terms of a dose: the more time your child or teen is online engaging with social media, the greater potential for developing a problem.

Crowding-Out Effect

Currently, children and teens spend an inordinate amount of time each day on a device of some kind. According to the Kaiser Family Foundation, kids between the ages of eight and 18 spent an average of 7.5 hours a day on a device for entertainment, roughly the equivalent of time spent working a full-time job. I don't fault kids for this and nor should you—devices are designed to be addictive and are quite effective at drawing and holding our attention.

Obviously, almost eight hours per day on a screen leaves room for little else. The crowding-out effect refers to exactly what it sounds like: time on devices crowds out opportunities for other activities, including those that contribute to well-being and positive mental health such as exercise, sports, hobbies, going outside, and spending time with family.

As a parent of a child or teen with a phone or a gaming system, I'm sure you know how hard it is to tear them away from screens. I bet you feel like you're in constant competition with that device for their attention, and you'd be right. I don't have to tell you how hard it can be to pull them off their devices and how much pushback they give you. Sometimes, it feels like it's just easier to avoid the fight and just let them stay on it.

I mentioned that screens crowd out time with family. Most of the kids I work with spend almost all of their time in their bedrooms on a device, either messaging people or just entertaining themselves. Spending time in one location (like a bedroom) also isn't good for kids' mental health. It's also hard to stay emotionally connected to a kid you hardly see, and that disconnection makes it far less likely your child will seek you out for support, comfort, or advice.

Sleep Deprivation

I suppose this could fall under the category of crowding out as well but it's more than just that. Many kids are allowed to keep their phones and laptops in their bedrooms, and they are often on those devices until very late at night thereby making it all but impossible to get enough sleep. In a study conducted by Common Sense Media, over half of kids (59%) used their phones on school nights well past midnight, spending their time primarily on various social media platforms to communicate with friends, watching videos on YouTube, or gaming.

In 2017, Jean Twenge conducted a study on how much time children and teens were sleeping relative to their social media use. She found that kids who use devices five or more hours a day were 50% more likely to get less than seven hours per night compared to those spending one hour a day on devices. Kids need more than seven hours of sleep every night (it's recommended that they sleep nine hours per night) and many get far less than that.

Sleep deprivation has a number of negative effects on children's physical and psychological well-being. The American Academy of Pediatrics has published an excellent report entitled, "Insufficient Sleep in Adolescents and Young Adults: Update on Causes and Consequences" that outlines the many negative effects of sleep deprivation, including increased irritability, drug and alcohol use, poor judgment, lack of motivation, poor academic performance, falling asleep in class, inattention, and depression.

The diagnosis of attention-deficit/hyperactivity disorder (ADHD) has increased significantly in the last decade, and in 2023, more people than ever before sought out medication for the treatment of ADHD. What I find interesting is that there is a great deal of overlap between the symptoms of ADHD and sleep deprivation. Both include difficulty concentrating, poor attention, slowed thinking, and difficulties regulating emotions.

I worked with a family who had a nonbinary 17-year-old who complained of not sleeping at night and having trouble staying focused in school. The parents took them to a psychiatrist who diagnosed ADHD and prescribed both a stimulant medication for the ADHD and a medication to help them with sleep. As it turns out, I learned that the kid was on their phone every night until very late, and on most nights, they were only getting about five hours of sleep. Once the parents fixed that (they required the kid to turn in their phone at 9:00 pm), both their sleeping and attention problems disappeared.

As you know, children and teenagers who don't get enough sleep are very hard to be around, especially in the mornings. They are not easy to wake up (who wakes up easily after only a few hours of sleep), they sleep through their alarm, and are super irritable—all of which starts the mornings off with conflict and arguments before sending them off to have a less-than-ideal school day. Later in the book, we'll talk about how to get kids up to an alarm, be in better moods, and be more self-sufficient in the morning.

Cyberbullying

The rates of children and teens who report having experienced cyberbullying have tripled since 2007. According to the Pew Research Center, almost half (46%) of U.S. teens ages 13–17 report online stalking, sexual harassment, body shaming, threats of violence, rumor spreading, and being cut out of friend groups.

It's these latter two—rumor spreading and being ostracized—that I tend to see most commonly in my practice (with sexual harassment for girls being a close third). It has become so easy to spread rumors online and manipulate others to exclude a kid such that they're banned from their friend group. It's such a painful experience for the child, and equally painful for a parent to witness (assuming, of course, that your child has told you about it in the first place). Once a kid has lost their social connections, especially if they are unable to regain them or make other friends, that becomes a recipe for developing depression and possible self-harm or suicidal thoughts. The impact of cyberbullying cannot be overstated, and it is shockingly common.

Furthermore, once a kid loses their friend group, they are often desperate to find another. However, often the new kids they connect with are not particularly good influences, thereby further eroding the child or teen's mental health. A kid desperately in search of a friend also becomes at risk for sexual predators and trafficking.

Unfavorable Social Comparisons

I won't spend too much time on this one because when people cite "social media" as the problem, this tends to be what they have in mind. It's true—most of us only post the good stuff online, giving the false impression that our own lives by comparison fall tragically short. This, of course, is an illusion that makes it seem like everyone else is better looking, richer, thinner, and having a lot more fun.

Psychologists call this upward social comparison, the tendency to judge our own worth by unfavorably comparing ourselves to others who we think have it better. While upward social comparison can sometimes motivate us to improve ourselves, more often it's just a recipe for unhappiness and low self-esteem.

Emotional and Behavior Contagion

This is an area that is often overlooked when we discuss the impact of screens on child and adolescent mental health.

Contagion refers to the process by which moods, emotions, and behavior are spread within social networks. By "networks," I mean social networks that are both virtual and in-person—basically anyone with whom you're in a relationship.

Nicholas Christakis and James Fowler have conducted extensive research on how behaviors and emotions spread within social networks. For an excellent overview of their work, you might take a look at Christakis's 2010 TED talk, "The Hidden Influence of Social Networks."

Many fascinating examples of social contagion exist in the research literature. For example, Christakis and Fowler found that if your friends are obese, your risk of becoming obese increases by 45%. Behavioral and emotional contagion have also been found for smoking, drinking, sleeping habits, loneliness, and more.

What makes this even more interesting is that not only do emotions and behaviors spread within your immediate social network, but you also spread them yourself into your other social networks. For example, if you're in a relationship with someone who is lonely or depressed, you are not only more likely to feel lonely or depressed yourself, but so are your friends' friends' friends (three degrees of separation). The effects of contagion tend to diminish with each degree of separation, finally reaching a point of unimportance after about three degrees. It's fascinating, isn't it? To think that you can adopt another person's emotions and behaviors simply by being in a relationship with them, and your friends will adopt those same emotions and behaviors simply because they're in a relationship with you.

Additionally, in a series of studies, Maya Rossignac-Milon and her fellow researchers describe a process that they refer to as merged minds. They argue that people in close relationships develop shared realties, i.e., the tendency to create connection and intimacy by gradually coming to see aspects of the world in the same, but not necessarily accurate, way. As this shared reality solidifies, those who are in that relationship tend to resist the influence or intrusion of competing ideas or beliefs of those external to the relationship. Sounds like our current political climate in the U.S., doesn't it?

Let me translate all of this into the world of teenagers and why this is important in our discussion of screens and social media.

Who your child or teen is in a relationship with, and what they talk about, will have powerful influences on your child's emotions and behaviors. These influences are often far more powerful than your own influence as their parent. We've all experienced the pull of our children's peer relationships. If our child is in a relationship with one or more friends who function well—don't get into trouble, are reasonably kind and respectful to their parents and others, go to school without much complaint, do their homework consistently, get decent grades, and so on—those friends are going to have a positive impact on your child. They'll build your kid up, encourage them not to make bad decisions, get their homework done, and most importantly be supportive and helpful to your kid when they encounter a problem or issue of some kind.

However, as you know, if your child or teen becomes friends with a less-than-ideal peer, that peer can have a profound negative impact or pull on your own kid. The other kid's moods or behaviors become socially contagious and increase the likelihood that your kid will behave in a similar way. If they are depressed, anxious, or angry, your kid might start to express those emotions as well.

When my colleagues and I work with a depressed and self-harming child or teen, we always want to know who their friends are and what they're talking about. What we find most of the time is that our patient is communicating with one or more friends who are also depressed, anxious, or suicidal. In addition, many times they are immersed in an unhelpful shared reality with one or more other kids. For example, together they have come to believe that self-harm makes them feel better, their parents don't understand them and can't help, therapy doesn't work, school is stupid, and so on. When we discover that this is happening, we always help the parents to take steps to mitigate the effects of these relationships. I'm going to circle back to how to do this in a bit when we talk about how to safely monitor kids' online activity.

Phones, tablets, and gaming systems make it extremely easy for kids to communicate with people who are not a positive influence. Sure, this can happen in person too, but relative to previous generations, Gen Z and Gen Alpha interact face-to-face with friends far less often. Instead, communication with friends is more often virtual, typically taking place in the child's bedroom, well out of earshot of their parents. Virtual relationships also open the door to meeting and communicating with others well beyond our children's own school and neighborhood, bringing them into contact with far-away strangers who may not have their best interests at heart.

Okay, hopefully, now you have a good understanding of why screens and other devices are playing such an important role in the mental health epidemic. In order to protect your child and buffer them against the negative influences of the dose-related effect, crowding out, sleep deprivation, cyberbullying, upward social comparison, and emotional and behavioral contagion, you're going to have to somehow put yourself in between your child and those darn devices.

Safely Mitigating and Monitoring Screen Time

Before I launch into this part of the chapter, here are a few quick caveats.

How much of this you end up doing is going to depend a lot on the kid that you have. Younger kids will need more monitoring and greater screen time limits than older kids, especially well-functioning older kids.

If you have an older teen and they are doing reasonably well—good kids who seem reasonably happy, getting chores done, doing their homework, honoring their curfew, are connected to a solid high-functioning peer group, and so on, you don't have to be as concerned with how much time they're on a device (within reason) and who they're talking to or what they're talking about. Concerned, yes, but not as concerned. Unless you have reason to be concerned about your child's mental health, such as a shift in their typical behaviors, the development of depressive or anxious symptoms, a change in their peer group for the worse, and so on, you probably can relax a bit.

An argument I often hear is that parents shouldn't be putting too many restrictions on kids' device time, or monitoring their virtual exchanges because it denies them the opportunity to acquire the self-regulation skills needed to best navigate their virtual lives. I agree with this to some degree, but with older kids who are clearly doing just fine.

However, I can't get behind this at all with younger kids. According to a study by Common Sense Media, 53% of kids in the United States have their own smartphones by age 11. I believe this is far too young without significant parental oversight, time restrictions, and monitoring content. Children of that age are simply too young and immature to be handed a fully enabled smartphone. Restrictions can be revisited periodically as the child gets older, more apps can be enabled, time limits extended, and less monitoring of exchanges and content as the kid demonstrates responsibility and positive mental health.

I simply cannot get behind this "let them learn by doing" strategy for any child or adolescent who has already developed symptoms of depression, anxiety, or self-harm/suicidal thoughts. Parents must intervene for all of the reasons described in this chapter.

Mitigating Strategy #1: Reducing Screen Time into the Relatively "Safe" Zone

We know that the amount of time on a screen each day (the dose-related effect) increases the potential for kids to develop a mental health condition (the risk of depression increases 13% for each additional hour on social media among adolescents). Furthermore, kids who spend less than three hours per day on social media have a lower probability of developing depressive symptoms than kids who spend more than five hours per day (18.1% versus 38.1%).

I strongly recommend that you limit your child's screen time to no more than one hour per day for kids 12 and under, and no more than three hours per day for teenagers (except for older teens (17 and above) or who are functioning pretty well.

This is, of course, easiest to start doing when your child or teen gets their first cell phone or gaming system, at which time they will likely agree to anything because they are so happy to get it. They very likely will complain about limited screen time and other restrictions as they get older, especially if their friends' parents don't have similar restrictions (which is likely). You can use the strategies we talked about earlier to avoid arguing about it, sidestep red herrings, and not getting into a tug-of-war. Just know that your kid won't like any of this but stand firm because it's the right thing to do.

There are many ways to make sure your child doesn't spend more than a few hours per day on a screen. Most phones have parental restrictions that you can put in place and monitor from your own phone that are reasonably effective. However, in my experience, not 100% effective, so you're going to need to get more familiar with the technology behind restrictions than maybe you care to. Kids are cagey with these restrictions too—they are highly motivated to circumvent them. You'll likely need to check periodically to make sure the screen time limits are still working because your kid for sure will never bring this to your attention if they are not.

This can be challenging for some parents, especially older parents who did not grow up with technology. However, it's well worth your time and attention, and while you may not ever become perfect at it, even a modest attempt at reducing screen time is far better than no attempt at all. Not to sound ageist in any way, but I've worked with plenty of grandparents who pull this off beautifully.

Parental controls also have the added benefit of allowing you to disable the phone remotely without having to physically take it away from your child or teen, which I do not ever recommend—that can go south very quickly with some kids and could get physical. It's best just to learn how to disable the phone remotely when you need to without asking for the device itself.

For devices besides a phone, such as gaming systems, laptops, tablets, and so on, it works best to configure your home's router to identify each device in your house connected to the internet so that you can selectively set time limits on how long the connection is enabled, as well as disable the connection automatically when you need to. Using your router in this fashion again allows you to disable devices without having physically to take them away.

Note that this strategy will not work for phones—simply cutting the internet connection to a phone with an enabled cell plan will do nothing. The cell service alone still allows the phone to be fully functional, which is why setting screen time limits via parental controls on the device itself is still necessary. An active cell plan also allows the kid to use a hotspot, which circumvents any restrictions you've tried to put on their Wi-Fi connection and allows then to still use laptops, tablets, and gaming systems. With some kids, I've found it's easiest to regulate screen time by not giving them a paid cell plan or pausing the one you have with your carrier until you feel the child is ready to have it safely returned.

Mitigating Strategy #2: Mitigating Crowding Out and Managing Pushback

We've also learned about the effects of crowding out, i.e., how excessive time on devices leaves little time for other wellness-enhancing activities. Many kids are on their phones and devices so much that they spend far less time out of their bedrooms interacting with family, getting exercise, doing homework, and so on.

If you take the steps to reduce your child or teen's screen time down to the three or fewer hours per day that I've recommended (the safe zone), they are going to have a lot more time each day to do other things that are good for them. However, if your child is already getting quite a bit more than three hours per day on a device, you're going to get pushback from them when you try to implement a reduction. Just know this is going to happen, it's inevitable, but there are some relatively simple steps you can follow to navigate the pushback.

First, try your best not to get into a back-and-forth argument when you first tell your child about reducing their screen time hours. Here is an explanation that you can use but don't expect it will be particularly persuasive:

> "I've been reading a lot lately about how too much time on a phone or other device isn't good for kids' mental health. I bet you've heard of this too. According to research, about three hours a day or less is probably safe but not more. This probably isn't your first choice, but I'd like you to start staying in those three hours. Thanks for that."

You're going to get red herrings galore ("None of my friends have screen time limits," "That's not true for me," "I've read other things that say screen time isn't bad"). You'll also likely be subjected to emotional pleas or bargaining to get you to change your mind, tantrums perhaps, and whatever else your child feels will be an effective way to deter you from taking this step. The resistance isn't going to last forever. Most kids let go of most of the fight within a week or two. However, the resistance will go on longer if you argue with them about it each time they bring it up, explain yourself over and over, appear uncertain, and by not sticking to the reduced hours consistently.

Just a quick note here. If your child or teen struggles with self-harm and suicide, it's not safe for you to take this step on your own. Anger at parents is often a precursor to self-harm. I do highly recommend that you still consider reducing screen time, but I strongly recommend that you find a competent therapist and let them walk you through the process safely otherwise it's too dangerous.

It's important that before you tell your child or teen you're not going to allow them to spend more than a few hours a day on a device, you're going to need to make sure you fully understand how to implement automatic screen time limits on your child's phone. You'll also need to know how to set a timer and remotely disable their Wi-Fi connection on your router. If you don't take time to learn these steps, your kid will always be one step ahead of you.

One of the things that seems to happen nearly all of the time once screen time is reduced is that your child will tell you they have nothing to do and they're bored. Sometimes, parents will fall into the trap of believing that it is their responsibility to keep the kid entertained since they are no longer on a device. Not so. Your kid is just rusty at finding other sources of entertainment, but they will eventually find something. If you find something for them, you're doing too much work on their behalf and you're denying them the opportunity to develop ways of keeping themselves occupied.

I also recommend that you don't make suggestions to them as to what they can do. Here's what will typically happen: they will swat away every idea you give them "boring," "dumb," or whatever. It's not really that they hate your ideas, of course, it's more about irritating you enough to give them more screen time hours. That's the function of the complaining. When your kid says, "Now what am I supposed to do!" the best response is, "I'm not sure, but I'm confident you'll find something." If you want to annoy them, play Joe's Walsh's song *Waffle Stomp* ("But don't let nobody tell you that there's nothin' to do").

Creating a Device-Free Time Period

This is a good alternative to adhering to the three hours per day screen time limit that some families often prefer. A device-free time period is a set time each day where everyone in the family, parents included, set their devices up on the kitchen counter and no one gets to pick them up. It's a great way for the entire family to unplug, and it shows kids that you're willing to suffer the pain of reducing your own screen time as well. I usually recommend a period of an hour and half or so on weekdays, usually around dinner time to entice kids to come to the dinner table. On weekends, I recommend three or four hours of device-free time both Saturday and Sunday.

I think you'll come to appreciate these screen time limits. Once you're no longer in competition with a device for your child's attention, kids have a way of magically wandering out of their bedrooms looking for something to do, and families often become that something. Watching a family movie together can be a screen time exception because you're all still together and interacting at least somewhat.

Here's one more cool thing you might observe once you reduce your kid's screen time: they'll be in a far better mood. My wife and I would sometimes not pay attention to how much time our youngest had been on her laptop. We paid the price for this because she would be in *a mood*. However, magically, once we told her to close her laptop, within minutes she's turned back into a human being who was far more enjoyable to be around.

Mitigating Strategy #3: Improving Sleep

I recommend that all screens and devices go off at least an hour before bedtime. This gives a kid's brain time to wind down and get ready for sleep. The blue light emitted from devices tricks the brain into thinking it's still daytime, which restricts the production of melatonin, a hormone involved in making us feel drowsy enough to fall asleep. I also recommend either remotely disabling all of their devices by way of a timer because it's really easy for parents to forget to collect devices or manually shut them off. In addition, I think it's better not to allow devices in the bedroom even if they've been disabled. I think for many kids it's just too tempting to spend that time trying to circumvent the restrictions. In addition, we get and respond to so many alerts on our phones every day that just having them nearby makes us tempted to pick them up to look at them out of sheer habit alone.

When you start all this in your family, again, your child will protest. They'll almost certainly tell you that they need their phone for their alarm or to play music to fall asleep. Both of these problems can easily be solved without a phone, so please don't be deterred.

Mitigating Strategy #4: Mitigating Social Contagion and Monitoring Online Exchanges

I highly recommend that you monitor your child or teen's online exchanges with others. This is one of the best ways to protect them from emotional and behavior contagion because you'll be able to see what your kid is saying to other people and what they're saying back to them. This allows you to intervene if you learn a relationship has become problematic or your child is communicating with someone who is a negative influence.

Another advantage of monitoring exchanges is that kids who are suicidal will often tell their friends about this before they tell their parents. In my clinical practice, there have been a number of times a suicide was prevented because the parents had taken steps to monitor their child or teen online activity.

There are several ways to monitor communication that don't involve you actually going through your child's phone. I recommend the third-party app Bark because it will automatically monitor these exchanges and send alerts to your phone if it detects problematic content. The alert will contain snippets of the exchange itself so it still affords the kid some online privacy. If you do install Bark on your kid's phone, I recommend that you be transparent about that because if you aren't, you'll be alerted to something and that will lead to an awkward conversation about how you acquired that information. Bark has its limitations too (it can't monitor some apps) but it's far better than nothing at all.

Leveraging Devices for Better Behavior

In my clinical practice, I've learned that using screens and other devices is one of the most effective ways to incentivize a child to engage in consistently better behavior. Just about every kid now has access to a screen of some sort, and it is the one thing that both young kids and teenagers value and want to access to. You can leverage other things too as I've mentioned, such as time with friends. However, kids don't see their friends every day so it's useful to have something at your fingertips whenever you need it.

As you'll see in the next chapters, leveraging devices will be a cornerstone for getting homework and chores done, as well as improving day-to-day respect and helping kids be less oppositional and reactive. It's such a powerful and flexible incentive that it's really all you need to shape kids' behavior if you leverage devices in an optimal way. I'm going to describe the process but break it down for younger kids and teenagers because it's used slightly differently for the two age groups.

Leveraging Screens for Younger Kids

I recommend that for younger kids (around 11 and under), that you set aside a specific time period each day in which the device in question can be accessed and only then. This approach also has the added benefit of making it easier to stick to screen time limits since the time in which devices are accessed can be more easily monitored and electronically limited.

I find that many parents of younger kids give them access to tablets and the like as a reward for completing some sort of task, such as doing a little homework, helping out around the house, and so on ("If you finish five math problems, I'll give to 15 minutes on your tablet."). I've never much cared for this approach because it brings with it some problems.

First, as you know, many kids are hard to pull off their devices, which means that there is the potential for conflict multiple times throughout the day. Second, it feels too transactional to me ("If you do this then I'll give you that"), which I think sends the kid the wrong message, i.e., that they only need to do something if there's something in it for them. I feel strongly that kids need to do things simply because they've been asked to do them even when there is no immediate reward. Third, kids will often start to wheel and deal with their parents in a way that doesn't feel right to me ("Well, how much time do I get for putting away the dishes?").

My way of looking at it is that kids need to do their homework, clean up their rooms, be nice to their parents, and so on because it's the right thing to do, not because of a promise of a reward. Life doesn't really work that way either—we still need to do things even if the reward is distant or perhaps even nonexistent.

What works better is to create a set time period in the early evening whereby the device is only earned after the child takes care of their responsibilities throughout the day. Typically, this includes homework, chores, or whatever else, coupled with treating their parents and siblings in a positive or at least neutral way. It's the same idea we've talked about previously in the book, i.e., responsibilities first, play second (the Premack principle). For kids who struggle with temper tantrums, or who are aggressive to their parents or siblings, a device can be earned only if those behaviors are absent prior to the time in which the device is made accessible.

Since devices can be earned each day, there is always an opportunity to earn them the very next day. ("I'm sorry but you haven't earned the iPad today, but I'm happy to let you have it tomorrow assuming things go well between now and then.") This setup also allows for effective if/then statements at the beginning of some sort of problem behavior ("If you expect to get on your tablet tonight then you're going to need to speak to me in a nicer way"). On occasion, when some kids learn they did not earn time on a device as a result of a behavioral challenge, they might get angry. When that happens, it can be effective to say, "Look I know it's frustrating that you didn't earn screens tonight, but you'll have the opportunity again tomorrow. You won't, however, if you don't make good choices tonight, starting right now."

Leveraging Screens for Teenagers

With teenagers, this strategy is modified a bit. What I find works best is establishing a routine in the family in which screens and devices are automatically disabled at night and only re-enabled by parents the next day once the teen has met all of their responsibilities. This approach is highly effective for kids who struggle with daily task completion.

For example, to motivate a kid to be ready for school on time (and to remove distractions that might slow them down in the morning), devices are only enabled once the kid is fully ready to walk out the door. In the afternoon, right after school, devices are disabled again and only re-enabled once chores and homework are completed. What's great about this is it allows you to completely back away from having to ask your teen to do their chores or their homework because they just know they won't get their phone or their gaming system enabled until they do (more on chores and homework a little later in the book).

If a kid has already earned their device and it's fully enabled but some other behavior problem arises, the device can still be easily leveraged. For example, let's say after you've enabled your teenager's phone you notice that their room still needs to be straightened. You wouldn't turn off their phone right then; instead, you'd just ask them to take care of it before they did anything else.

However, if after a reasonable amount of time (15–30 minutes), it becomes clear that your teen isn't cleaning their room, then you'd disable their phone until the room is cleaned (pause, earn, and return reinforcement). In this scenario, when you disable their screens, as soon as the kid figures out that you've done this, most kids will come out of their room and ask why you turned their screens off. I'm sure they already know why, but a good response would be, "Because I asked you to clean up your room and you didn't. Get that taken care of please and call me when I can come take a look at it, then I'd be happy to re-enable your screens." Remember, don't argue, just say it matter-of-factly, and don't ask them to clean their room a second time. It might take a kid a while to get started, or they might start it but stop again, but just wait them out because they know that's the only way their devices will be turned back on.

Now that you have a handle on screens, both how to remotely disable them and how to leverage them for better behavior, let's take a look at other common behavioral challenges and what to do about them.

Chief takeaways from Chapter 9

- Time on screens and devices presents an odd paradox. Devices have tremendous potential to harm kids, but if safely managed, they can be used as very powerful change agents in your family.
- Screen time is one of the largest contributors to the current childhood mental health epidemic. Reducing and monitoring time on devices alone will help buffer your child from developing a mental health challenge.
- Devices bring with them negative influences that include the dose-related effect, the crowding-out effect, sleep deprivation, cyberbullying, unhelpful social comparisons, and emotional and behavior contagion.
- Many of the influences can be safely mitigated by parents, such as limiting screen time to no more than three hours per day (the safe zone) and using a third-party app to monitor both your child or teen's content and online communications.
- Consider the use of a device-free time period each day to reduce the entire family's screen time and draw kids out of their bedrooms.
- Once you've taken the steps to reduce and monitor time on devices, they can now be used to leverage very effectively all kinds of positive behavior, from getting chores and homework done to treating you in a kind, respectful way.

Part IV

Common Challenges and How to Solve Them

Helping Your Child or Teen Be More Respectful and Follow Your Directions

10

Two of the most common issues that come up in my practice when I work with parents with oppositional kids are being spoken to in a disrespectful way and the child or teen not doing what they've been asked to do. Sometimes, the two behaviors go hand in hand but not always; however, both can become major flashpoints and a source of ongoing stress and conflict. Learning how to respond effectively both to disrespect and oppositional behavior in a way that improves these behaviors can make a world of difference.

Before we get into the meat of this, and before you attempt to address your child or teen's disrespect, you're going to need to make sure your side of the street on this is really clean. By that I mean if you want them to be kind and respectful to you or anyone else, you first have to model that yourself for them. Be who you want them to be. You don't have to be perfect, obviously, but if most of the time you lean toward treating your child with kindness and respect, if that's your factory setting so to speak, you'll retain your moral authority when you expect them to do the same for you.

Disrespect and Cursing

Disrespect can take many forms in kids, but most of the time it's something the kid says. In general, disrespect includes being spoken to by your child or teen in a way that isn't okay, such as yelling or screaming at you; speaking to you in a harsh, mean, or sarcastic tone; interrupting you or talking over you (especially when you're trying to say something that they don't want to hear); shutting down conversations in an angry way; ordering you to leave their bedroom; and so on.

DOI: 10.4324/9781003452638-14

Cursing obviously falls into this category as well. Kids can vary quite a bit in terms of the degree to which this is a problem, and families vary quite a bit in terms of their tolerance for cursing. We tend to think of cursing as more of a problem with teenagers and usually it is, but I've worked with quite a few little kids who think nothing of dropping the f-bomb in front of their parents (or their grandparents, teachers, and pretty much everyone else). I've also worked with many teenagers who are massively disrespectful to their parents, but they never curse at them.

We should also distinguish kids who just curse around their parents from kids who curse directly at their parents. I think this is a really important distinction because there are a lot of parents who are reasonably okay with their kids cursing ("Oh fuck!"), but I've never met a parent who is okay with their kids cursing at them ("Fuck you!"). I know I'm probably biased and obviously every family gets to make their own decision on this, but I prefer kids not to curse at all in front of their parents because it just seems to open the door to the eventual "fuck you." I'll address both types of cursing in this chapter in case you decide not to allow either kind in your family.

It's also important to distinguish disrespect from general irritability or grumpiness. Parents will sometimes see this as disrespect and respond in a less-than-ideal way. We're all human and have bad days, kids especially, so I generally don't recommend intervening much on irritability as long as it's not directed at you or someone else. I think what works best is just to give the kid a wide berth and some space. We can generally tell when our kids are in bad moods. For example, say your teen comes into the kitchen first thing in the morning. You're probably going to say "Good morning" or something like that and maybe even try to make some kind of small talk. I think you'll know pretty quickly what kind of a mood your kid is in, and if you get a sense they're irritable, just quietly leave them alone and don't try to initiate more conversation (and certainly don't call them out on the irritability in a stern way).

If you give a kid some time and space, their mood will eventually improve all on its own. Kids' moods can vary wildly over the course of a single day (or even a single hour); that's really normal. Remember too that it's not necessarily your job to fix their bad mood or find out what's bugging them. Sometimes, I see parents who anxiously fret when their child or teen is in an irritable mood and the parent feels the need to "help" them with it. Typically, this includes asking the kid over and over what's wrong and hovering over them which is a surefire way to make someone even more irritable. Of course, it's okay to notice your kid's bad mood, and I find it works best to just very gently say, "Are you okay? You don't seem like yourself today." Most kids will respond with a "Nothing's wrong" or "I'm fine," but the mere act of noticing and posing the question results in a softening of their mood (which also works great with adults too).

A mood that lingers beyond a day or so, yes, you'd want to try and gently open a dialog about that because it suggests there really is something important on their mind.

Let's circle back to disrespect. I think one of the things that is most helpful when it comes to managing disrespect is for parents to establish a culture within their family early on when kids are little that speaking disrespectfully isn't okay. I don't think kids, including young kids, should bark at their parents or raise their voices in anger, nor should their parents do the same to them. We can be angry with someone and not yell at them. With younger kids, in most situations, a response to this can be as simple as, "It's not okay to talk to me that way," or "Look, I get that you're angry but I'm not happy with how you're speaking to me right now." I would never try to problem-solve or negotiate with a kid who continued to talk to me in a disrespectful way. It's better to disengage and walk away after saying something like, "Let me know when you're ready to talk without yelling please."

I've found that with most younger kids, this response is often enough. However, for kids who persist in the disrespect (keep yelling and/or saying mean things), I'd either ask them to go to their rooms for a while until they can be nicer, or I'd make an if/then statement ("If you want to get on your tablet or watch TV tonight, I'm going to need you to talk to me in a nicer way please."), interventions covered in previous chapters. It's really important that you always respond to disrespect in a way that reduces the probability of it happening again and that you send your kids a clear message that disrespect isn't acceptable. Don't just keep telling your kid over and over to be more respectful; that doesn't work. Instead, as we've talked about before, you're going to need to give them a reason to change their behavior.

The strategy for navigating disrespect with preteens and teenagers is very similar and follows this same basic strategy. If your teenager starts to speak to you in a disrespectful way, you'd want to say something like, "Whoa, not okay. I'm happy to talk but not when you talk to me that way. Dial it back please." The "dial it back please" is a cue, which means you're asking them to rewind what they just said and say it again but in a better way. I think when it comes to general disrespect, it's good to cue the kid once and give them a chance for a do-over.

If that doesn't work and they don't dial it back you'd just matter-of-factly impose whatever consequences are a part of your family's routine. For a younger kid, that might include being asked to go to their rooms for a short while. For a teenager, it would include shutting off their devices until they've been nice to you for a while, maybe just a few hours for mild disrespect and a day or two for more serious disrespect (pause, earn, and return). Serious examples of cursing (e.g., "Fuck you! or "You're a bitch!") would result in not earning screens or devices that day but could be earned again the next day assuming the teen's behavior is positive between now and then. I think this type of cursing is serious and will likely only stop by heavily leveraging devices by using pause, earn, and return.

Some kids who have been disrespectful and/or cursed at you for many years are going to need some time and effort on your part to reduce these behaviors. Again, it always starts with setting the expectation ("It's not okay to curse in our family") and then imposing room time or device restrictions over and over, probably for at least a month or two (sometimes longer) before you start seeing results. *[Note: again, if your kid is physically aggressive or self-harms, you should work with a therapist to help you implement this strategy in a safe manner.]*

Oppositional Behavior and Not Following Directions

As I've mentioned before in the book, I think it's very important that when you ask your child or teen to do something, they should do it. Of course, pick your battles, and try not to engage in a needless tug-of-war, but it's important to follow through on your expectations or requests otherwise the kid learns requests made of them are optional. Often, as we've talked about, the function of oppositional behavior is task avoidance. When a kid doesn't want to do something and you let them off the hook from doing it because they've been disrespectful or oppositional, you're reinforcing the wrong behavior and just teaching your child that being oppositional works.

A family sent me a video clip of an interaction between a 12-year-old boy and his mother. He was sitting at the kitchen table allegedly doing his homework, but in reality he was watching YouTube videos. The mom did the right thing in that she very calmly asked him to change seats so that his laptop screen was facing outward. He didn't like that idea very much and began to argue and threw red herrings at her. ("Why do I have to change seats when I'm just doing my homework?") Unfortunately, she responded to each red herring, which only further incentivized the boy to push back even harder, gradually becoming disrespectful and yelling at his mom to go away and leave him alone.

Unfortunately, she did just that—she went quiet and walked away just as he ordered her to do.

I know earlier in the book I said that when kids start to yell at you, it's best to disengage and walk away. However, not in situations like this one. By complying with his demands that she leave the room, she reinforced both the disrespect and the oppositional behavior, essentially teaching him that if he's forceful enough with her he won't have to do what's been asked. As soon as she left the room, predictably, he immediately calmed down but never ended up having to change seats.

I'd like you to pause here please before reading further. Take a few moments to think about this scenario and test yourself now that we've come this far in the book. See if you can come up with a different response to the boy when he said that he would not change seats. Let's make it challenging: what could you say that would have resulted in him changing seats and not yelling at you? See if you can do that using just two sentences. You'll get the most out of this book by trying to come up with your own response before I tell you in the next paragraph as people learn best that way.

Here's the answer (or my answer anyway). When the boy first asks why he needs to change seats, this following response would stand a pretty good chance of working: "I've already told you why and I'm not going to argue about it (grey rock). If you expect to use your Xbox tonight, you need to finish your homework and sit where I've asked you to (an if/then statement)." The mom should then turn around and walk away because as we've learned, if/then statements don't produce an immediate positive result; you must disengage and give the kid a few minutes to think it over. Sit back and let the contingency do its job. This response also avoids the tug-of-war this mom found herself in as now she's let go of the rope. If the boy changes seats, problem solved. If he doesn't change seats, then he'll not earn his device time later that day and that's his choice to make.

For teenagers, pause, earn, and return reinforcement is the most effective way to ensure that kids do what's asked of them. Phones and other screens are so powerfully motivating that simply turning those off until the task at hand has been completed works well with most oppositional kids ("I'm happy to turn your phone back on once your room has been picked up"). This strategy is so much more effective than using punishment ("You didn't clean your room so now you've lost your phone for a week."). All that would do is give you an angry kid who still has a messy room. Occasionally, a kid will tell their parents that they don't care if they turn off their phone or disconnect their W-Fi connection, but I've found that in most cases this is just bravado and they most definitely do care. The best response to this is a simple "Okay" and just quietly wait them out. It's the rare kid that will go days and days without screens before finally just agreeing to pick up their room or whatever was asked of them. You'll find throughout the rest of this book that we're going to apply this same strategy to many other situations.

Often, kids say "You can't make me do it," and a good response to that is "That's true, you'll either do it or you won't." If a kid decides not to do something and earns the consequence, they're perfectly free to make that decision. Tomorrow is another day, of course, and he'll have another opportunity to earn devices but only after he's done his homework and sat where he's been asked.

I've also learned that when you ask a kid to do something, but you think there's a possibility they might not do it, your demeanor when you make the ask matters a lot. Sometimes, what works really well is when you ask a child or teen to do something, you do it in a very casual way, almost giving off an air or vibe that you're fully confident that they'll do it. You say it in a very easy and relaxed way, often without even making eye contact, and often the kid just magically does it. However, if the uncertainty leaks out in your tone of voice or body language, the kid takes this as a cue that even you don't believe they're going to do it.

Along these same lines, one of the interesting things about very strong-willed, highly oppositional children and teens is how often they'll follow a direction if you just leave them alone. After giving a request, pause and wait a bit because many kids need about 30 seconds or so to fully process a request. It might look like resistance or that they're ignoring you, but really they're processing. Often when saying nothing more, about 30 seconds later many kids will slowly get up and turn off the TV, or whatever the request. This can serve to avoid a lot of unnecessary conflict, especially when parents respond with "I said now!"

I worked with the parents of a 14-year-old girl who, when asked to do something by either parent, would immediately say no. I think she was just in the habit of doing this and probably said no to everything, almost as a reflex. What was interesting about this family is that the mom responded to the "no" much differently from the dad. For example, if she asked her daughter to set the table for dinner, the girl would always say no, but the mom learned that if she said nothing in response and didn't look at her, the kid almost always complied within a few minutes. However, when the dad asked her to do something, she would also say no to him, but then he would get into it with her ("Don't argue with me, I'm not going to tell you again!"). Predictably, through the principles of mirroring and matching and tug-of-wars, his approach would escalate into heated conflict, and the kid rarely ended up doing anything her dad asked.

Let's move on now to other kinds of problematic behavior and see if we can figure out what to do to improve them.

Chief takeaways from Chapter 10

- Disrespect and problems following directions are often major flash-points and sources of conflict in families raising a strong-willed child.
- Disrespect generally includes kids yelling at their parents, saying something in a harsh, sarcastic, or mean way, interrupting or talking over them, and so on.
- It can also include cursing. Some families are okay with mild cursing, but kids cursing directly at their parents is never acceptable.
- If the disrespect or cursing persists when you try walking away, or if the disrespect is more serious or hurtful, then leveraging privileges becomes important ("If you expect to be on your phone or tablet tonight, I need you to talk to me in a nicer way please.")
- For teenagers engaging in milder disrespect, it can be very helpful to cue them once before going straight to leveraging devices ("Whoa, dial it back please and try that again.")
- Kids need to do what's asked of them, otherwise they'll come to believe that following your directions is optional.
- The most effective way to help kids do what's asked of them is to use pause, earn, and return reinforcement rather than punishment ("Once your room is picked up, I'd be happy to turn your phone back on.")

Starting the Day in the Right Way

11

How to Have More Peaceful Mornings

I'm going to devote an entire chapter to the subject of morning routines because it's the rare family that comes into my office that doesn't bring this up at some point as a major source of conflict.

If you think about it, it makes sense that strong-willed and oppositional kids would have problems in the morning because look at all the things that they're being asked to do that, in truth, no one really wants to do. They must wake up not when they want to, but at some hour that is usually well before any of us really wants to wake up. Next, they have do get a lot of things done, none of which are even remotely fun or interesting. This includes getting dressed, brushing their teeth and other kinds of hygiene-type things, eating breakfast when they may or may not be hungry, taking medication (maybe), getting their backpacks together, and finally walking out the door for school, all under a time crunch supervised by well-meaning parents who are in a hurry and barely awake. Mix into that a kid who is oppositional by nature, or a child or teen with attention-deficit disorder.

What could possibly go wrong?

Here's how all of this plays out in most families to greater or lesser degrees. First, the kid is hard to wake up so parents by default become human alarm clocks. They try to be pleasant and cheerful when they go into their child or teen's bedroom because they've learned that there's a high probability that their kid will resist getting up, try to fall back asleep, and bite their head off in the process. Some parents try to wake their kid up in stages—first by going into the room and telling them it's time to get up, leaving and returning a few minutes later to open the blinds, leaving and returning to ask what they want for breakfast, and so on.

Finally, when the kid gets out of bed, they move onto endlessly coaxing them through their routine, with each task in the process becoming another source of resistance and conflict. Many kids drag their feet or get

DOI: 10.4324/9781003452638-15

stalled in spots along the way, thereby forcing parents to start nagging, getting pulled into a tug-of-war, and ultimately even losing their temper. Last, it's finally time to walk out the door so the kid can get to school on time. Oops, the backpack is nowhere to be found and likely last night's homework never made it inside so there's a big last-minute scramble to find it.

Rinse and repeat, Monday through Friday. This is clearly not a recipe for anyone to start their day off in a good mood, ready to take on the world.

This scenario is, of course, the opposite of what every parent wants. We all hope for relaxed, peaceful mornings. If the kid is old enough to get up to an alarm, you'd like them to do so without hitting the snooze button over and over. In a perfect world, you'd just generally be around as you watch them go through their morning routine, more or less independently with little or no nudging from you. You can get ready yourself in a leisurely way, drink your coffee, and enjoy your morning. When it's time to go, the backpack is ready by the door, everyone is in a good mood, and with time to spare.

I bet that seems like a dream, right?

I've learned over the years, both with the kids who I've worked with, and raising my own four daughters, that an ideal morning like this is doable, but there's a science to it, and a little sprinkle of art as well.

Thankfully, I was able to get a lot of practice at pulling off peaceful morning routines when I worked with kids living in residential treatment programs, almost all of whom were strong-willed and oppositional. The shift that I worked required that I wake up six kids, see them through their routines (hygiene, chores, medication, breakfast, etc.), and drive them all to school hopefully on time. The hard part about school was that none of them were the same ages or went to the same schools, and none of them could ride the bus.

Here are a few things that helped a lot, which can be applied to just about any kid. First, whatever amount of time you think your child or teen needs to get ready in the morning moving at a leisurely pace, get them up about a half an hour earlier than that. Mornings are more peaceful when no one is rushed, and so you want to build in plenty of time for things to go wrong, like not finding an article of clothing, someone monopolizing the bathroom, or a forgotten homework assignment. By making mornings ridiculously long, no matter what unexpected thing arises, you'll still have time for it and not be rushed. I've known kids who roll out of bed only 10 minutes before they leave for school, so of course they're rushing and the smallest hiccup blows up the entire morning.

Second, complete as many tasks as you can the night before. It teaches preplanning, and the value of not leaving things until the last second. Backpacks should be fully ready to go with homework inside, parked right next to the front door ready to grab as your kid walks out. Younger kids can pick out their clothes the night before if that helps. In terms of breakfast, some kids just aren't hungry in the morning so there's no need to battle over getting them to eat something. I find this is the one thing that parents stress about the most in the morning but despite what they say I don't think breakfast is really all that important, and they'll do just fine in school. Though nutritionists might disagree, they don't have to ready a challenging kid for school. It is just not worth ruining a morning over, risking peace and flow and getting them off to a good positive start to their day. If you're worried about it though, you can keep something in their backpacks if they get hungry later.

Third, capitalize on the Premack Principle. You'd want to hold all the fun stuff for the very end, such as breakfast (if they like breakfast), watching TV, or time on a tablet or other device until they've completed absolutely every other task. ("You're welcome to watch TV as soon as you're completely read to go.") I've known some parents who let their younger kids watch TV or go on YouTube while they are getting dressed. If this is working for you that's totally okay, but I find most kids just stall in front of a screen. Withholding the screen, however, gives them a reason (a motivator) to keep moving through their routine at a decent pace.

Speaking of moving, your goal is to teach your child to become independent in the morning. One parent who I worked with was still picking out clothes for her 13-year-old because "He has a hard time making decisions." That might be true, but he's never going to get better at making decisions if he has someone make them for him. I think you might be surprised just how much your child or teen can do on their own in the morning without your involvement and with the right incentives in place. Let the incentives do the work for you. The kid knows that the only way they can access screens is to be ready on time, so there's no need to remind them what to do next as that just opens the door to more resistance. However, if you think your child has legitimately lost track of time, it's okay to give them a gentle reminder when needed.

Getting up to an Alarm

I've learned that almost any kid can wake up to an alarm, starting as young as about five years old. However, it's the rare oppositional kid, including older teenagers, who actually does. Most commonly, both the parents and the teen say the same thing, which is that they've tried to get the kid up to an alarm but they "just sleep through it" or they shut it off and go back to sleep.

There are two reasons for this generally. First, for many kids, they have problems waking up in the morning because as we've talked about before, they were up too late the night before, usually on their phones or another device. I've discussed the effects of screen time on sleep earlier in the book and how to mitigate these influences. Often, once kids are off their screens at least an hour before bedtime, problems waking up in the morning are vastly improved. Once kids start getting enough sleep, they wake up far more easily in the morning and are much less irritable. Don't be dissuaded by your teen telling you that they need their phone to listen to music in bed or use it as their alarm, both problems can be easily remedied in ways that don't involve using their phone.

The second problem that gets in the way of kids waking up to an alarm is a motivation issue. Often, they don't see any reason to get up to an alarm because they know their parents will just wake them up. Parents also become the de facto snooze button in that they wake up the kid, the kid goes back to sleep for 10 more minutes, parents wake them up again, the kid falls back asleep, and so on.

I highly recommend that if your child or teen isn't currently getting up to an alarm that you consider putting a plan into place to make that happen. Some kids will work very hard to talk their parents out of it, but I've yet to meet one kid who couldn't do this eventually. If they tell you that it's impossible for them to get up to an alarm, just remind them that you have every confidence that they can and everyone learns how to do it eventually.

Leveraging More Powerful Incentives for a Better Morning Routine

If you've tried the interventions that I've suggested so far to improve your child's mornings, such as building in extra time, getting as much done as you or they can the night before, using the Premack Principle, and if they still are having problems and/or refusing to get up to their alarm, it's time for more leverage.

For a younger child, you might consider following the same strategy outlined in the previous chapter, i.e., setting aside time in the evening when screens can only be earned on days in which they've had a great morning. This opens the door for using an if/then statement as well if a snag starts to develop in the morning, such as "If you'd like to use your tablet tonight, I'm going to need you to be ready to walk out the door on time today please."

For older kids and teenagers, cell phones and access to screens is almost always enough to counteract a motivation problem. I recommend that parents first start by sitting down with their kid and talking through the morning routine problem. ("Things seem tense and rushed in the mornings. Have you noticed that too? How about we look for things we can all do to make that better.") This is a good time to ask that they start to get up to an alarm or make sure that their backpack is ready to go by the door. Some kids respond just fine to this approach and are reasonably collaborative, but most parents who I work with have already tried it without success. Many oppositional kids are open to the conversation and agree to do things differently, but most of the time things stay exactly the same.

I recommend that parents still try this approach again (a conversation) even if it hasn't worked, but I'll ask them to add one more sentence at the end: "Why don't we try this for a week and then evaluate how it's going?" If nothing has changed after a week, then you can sit down with your teen again, but now it's time to give them a heads-up on what's coming next. It flows like this:

PARENT (P): Hey, what happened this week? We had talked about you getting up to your alarm by 7:00 and being ready to walk out the door no later than 8:30.

CHILD (C): I tried.

(P): I recall us having to wake you up every morning.

(C): You know I can't get up to an alarm. I'm a heavy sleeper. *[NOTE: That's a red herring, obviously.]*

(P): Well, I know it's not your favorite thing to do, or mine. But you did agree, didn't you?

(C): I only agreed to try.

(P): I see. How about this? Let's give it another week, but if you're still not consistently getting up to your alarm and

	we're walking out the door late, I think that should be a day you don't take your phone to school.
(C):	WAIT, WHAT?
(P):	And I'd be happy to give it back to you the next day, assuming you're up to your alarm and out the door on time then.
(C):	That's not fair. You know I need my phone at school. *[NOTE: To my knowledge, schools do not require kids to have phones nor do they really "need" to have phones, so don't fall for that.]*
(P):	Well, fair or not, that's what I'm going to do. And, of course, the consequence is entirely avoidable, but I'll let you decide how you're going to handle it. Thanks for listening.

Most kids would do just about anything to take their phone to school. If the phone isn't a big draw for them (for some kids it just isn't), something else probably will be, such as gaming with their friends ("I'd only be okay with you gaming at night on the days in which you're up to your alarm and ready to leave on time.").

I like targeting just those two things: up to an alarm and walking out the door on time. That seems to also cover everything in between. It addresses two separate problems, i.e., the reluctance to get up to an alarm and the foot dragging in the morning. Again, you don't need to prod a kid along in the morning because it's their job to do what's needed to leave on time and to move through the steps without your help. Resist the temptation to nag and let the contingency (the phone) do the work for you.

Of course, it goes without saying (but I'll say it anyway), that if your kid doesn't hold up their end of the bargain in the morning, you must follow through and deliver the consequence. Otherwise, the intervention won't work because they won't take you seriously. It's important to know as well that for some kids just the idea of losing their phone is enough for them to change their behavior, but for most kids they likely will need to experience the consequence, possibly more than once, to start changing their behavior so that mornings become a more peaceful experience for everyone.

Chief takeaways from Chapter 11

- Mornings are typically challenging for oppositional kids and can be a source of almost daily conflict.
- Understandably so. Mornings require kids to do all kinds of things that aren't particularly fun, such as getting up early, taking care of their hygiene, and so on, all while being rushed.
- Ideally, kids should be able to wake up to an alarm and move themselves independently through each task with only minimal help from you. This is entirely doable for the vast majority of kids.
- Small changes in the routine can be helpful, such as adding an extra 30 minutes each day to get ready in case there's a snag, completing as many tasks as possible the night before, and making use of the Premack Principle (allowing screens and other fun stuff only after everything else is done).
- Almost every kid from about the age of five and up can get up to an alarm despite what your kid might be telling you.
- Leveraging screens can be very helpful to motivate kids to have better mornings. For younger kids, that might be something like, "You can use your tablet any evening that you have a good morning." For older kids and teenagers, that might be "You're welcome to take your phone to school any day you're up to your alarm and out the door on time."

No More Arguments and Bickering Between Siblings 12

Of course, if your child or teen doesn't have any siblings, this chapter likely won't be of much interest to you. However, if they do, I'm guessing you are frequently intervening on squabbles and find this to be both challenging and a frequent source of stress and conflict in your family.

I'm going to start off by letting you know that arguing between siblings is actually really common and for the most part falls into the "normal" range of behavior. I suspect that this is just what kids do because it's so common, and the behavior itself looks more or less the same between one family and the next. When I was growing up, my brothers and I fought constantly, both verbally and physically, and I know it drove my parents up the wall. We never meant any harm to each other, we usually made up within minutes, and most of the time we got along just fine, until, of course, we didn't.

I'm going to propose several reasons why bickering between siblings is common and let's see if any of them resonate with you.

First, I've long suspected that the behavior itself is hardwired in human beings, as it probably is in other primates. Playing among kids, and teasing each other for fun, might be an important component of the attachment process and maintaining social connections. I remember a story that I heard in graduate school about a group of young chimpanzees in a cage. There were chickens nearby, and the chimps would slowly try to lure one over to their cage by throwing out small scraps of food. When the chicken got close enough, one of the chimps would poke a sharp stick through the bars of the cage to startle the chicken and make it fly away, at which point all the chimps would burst out laughing. (It's true chimpanzees laugh.) The chimps would have endless fun because, sadly, the chickens never caught onto the game and wised up. So, teasing might be part of our DNA.

DOI: 10.4324/9781003452638-16

I'm guessing as well that young kids are always testing out and jockeying for position on the social hierarchy. Someone always has to be on top, and the one who isn't would love to be there. Most of the bickering that I've observed between siblings seems to be about who's on first: "It's my toy and not yours," "It's my turn to pick the movie and not yours," "I'm right and you aren't," and so on. And, as I'm sure you're aware, kids will fight about anything, no matter how small or apparently trivial the issue. It's good to be king and no one wants to be dethroned, especially by a younger brother or sister.

I also believe that fights between siblings can serve as a form of entertainment, especially when kids are bored. That probably was the case with the chimpanzees, and I know my brothers and I were more likely to bicker and fight when we ran out of things to do. It was just *so much fun* and highly entertaining as long as it wasn't my turn to be on the receiving end of it or our parents ruined it by stepping in.

I'm telling you all of this because I think sometimes parents worry that there might be something wrong with their kids if they argue and fight a lot, or sometimes maybe even get physical with each other. That being said, a kid who routinely bullies a sibling (as some strong-willed kids will do), or if it often comes to blows between your kids, while different in nature, the interventions to address these are pretty much still the same.

Don't worry either if your kids say they hate each other. They probably do sometimes, but certainly not all of the time, no matter what they tell you. It's also really common for siblings who loved spending all of their time together as younger kids to drift apart during adolescence, but it's been my observation that in most cases because they still love each other, the relationship tends to get better again in early adulthood.

So, what do we do about all the fighting?

Schools of Thought

There are generally two common ways of addressing this problem, but I've never found either to work particularly well.

Let's call the first one the "let them work it out" approach. I think the idea here is that kids should be given an opportunity to solve the conflict of the moment themselves without a whole lot of parental intervention. This is more of an old-school approach, and I don't think it works well at all. If you've ever seen two kids fighting about something, and it almost seems to escalate, the probability of two angry kids suddenly arriving at an equitable solution and then shaking on it seems quite low to me. I've learned that not intervening actually increases the chances of an argument turning physical, and then it's a real mess.

I'll call the second school of thought the "teach kids the skills they need to resolve their differences" approach. Part of this is obviously a really good thing—kids are often terrible at conflict resolution and teaching them how to talk things through and negotiate their differences is a great life skill. I think every parent should make some effort to teach these skills; it's just common sense, but I don't think that alone is going to keep your kids from bickering in the first place. If bickering is a form of entertainment or a way to move up in the dominance hierarchy, where is the incentive or motivation to use skills and stop fighting? I feel that if you've done your best to teach your kids conflict resolution skills and they're just not having any of it, especially in situations in which they're getting really aggressive and not listening to you, it's time to change your approach.

I don't think it's okay for kids to bicker with each other. By "bickering," I mean that back-and-forth thing kids do ("It's mine! No, it's mine!"). We've all seen married couples who bicker too, and this is the word we use to describe that same behavior. The exchanges seem small and petty, and not really about anything, which is exactly what kids do too.

If I hear kids start to bicker, I'll listen to a few of those exchanges (I guess my abbreviated version of the "let them work it out" approach) and maybe let them trade a few sentences back and forth. If it doesn't stop there, I'll intervene because I've learned that if I don't stop it myself, it's very likely it is going to get worse. It's far easier to disrupt bickering earlier in the anger escalation cycle rather than later, so I'd want to jump in when I still have the best chance of disrupting and putting an end to the conflict.

First, Here's What Doesn't Work

I don't think it's at all helpful to try and figure out who started it. Two kids will never agree on this and insist the other was at fault. I'm sure you know what happens when you attempt this: one kid will start by blaming the other, the second kid starts to talk over them and defend themselves, and so on to the point where neither is listening to you anymore—they've just gone back to bickering again.

One of the cool things about using the word "bickering" is that it is "fault-neutral." It doesn't really matter who started it; what matters is that they are now both doing the bickering. It's the bickering that you call them out on, not the thing that actually started it, and it's pretty clear that both kids are now participating. So, if a kid says it's not their fault it's the other kid's, you'd want to say, "It doesn't matter to me who started it. You're both bickering now, and you know that's not okay."

However, if it's very clear to me that one kid really did start it, or if they have a pattern of instigating things as some oppositional kids do, rather than using the approach I'm going to describe below, you'd want to handle it differently. For a kid who has a pattern of instigating things with siblings, I'd want to make it clear to them that any privileges (e.g., time on devices or seeing friends) are only going to be available to them on a day in which they haven't fought with their siblings. Any sort of egregious behavior, such as bullying, will for sure result in no device time or other privileges that day and possibly beyond.

What to Do

The first thing I recommend that you say is, "You guys, stop bickering please" without raising your voice, and in a matter-of-fact, neutral way.

In a perfect world, this is how you'd get any behavior to stop, right? All you'd have to do is say, "Please don't do that," and the negative behavior would magically end and never come back. I know it doesn't work this way with your oppositional kid, or at least not yet anyway. With easy-to-parent children and teens, this is often the only intervention needed, and the kids will just do as you asked.

However, even with harder kids, I'm hoping that we can get your kid to respond in exactly this same way. I suspect what has made this harder in your family is that as we've discussed, you can tell a kid over and over to do something or stop doing something, but without a way to back up that expectation, many kids just don't listen. This book is all about how to back up what you say, using interventions such as staying matter-fact, disengaging, making if/then statements, asking not commanding, leveraging devices, using pause, earn, and return reinforcement, and so on. Eventually, over time, by using these interventions and getting good at them, what you say will finally start to matter again, and when say "please don't do that," your kid will listen and stop because they'll know exactly what your next response will be if they don't.

The same thing will happen with, "You guys stop bickering please" because if they don't, here's what will happen next.

Separating and Time in Bedrooms

It seems to me that the one thing siblings really want deep down is to be in the same room with each other. Not always, of course, but often. They might not act like it, or show it necessarily, but I do think in their hearts that's really what they want. This seems especially true if they've been separated for a while, which is the underlying principle behind sending kids to their rooms to stop them from bickering.

We've covered the mechanics of sending kids to their bedrooms earlier in this book. You'll have wanted to set up the long/short thing in advance and are hopefully using it regularly. Then, when you ask your children or teens to go their rooms for bickering, they'll do so fairly easily most of the time because they know they'll be in there longer if not. Even a very short amount of time separated in bedrooms is often enough to disrupt the bickering and put an end to it.

Many kids, especially younger kids, can't stop bickering on their own, which is why you step in and need to put an end to it on their behalf.

If you've said, "You guys, stop bickering please," it's best to give them a moment or two to actually stop. Like if/then statements, it can take a few seconds for what you said to actually register. It's also true that it might sink in with one kid faster than the other, and if that's the case, you've solved half your problem and only one kid is still doing the bickering.

If it doesn't stop, you'd want to say this, "I'd like you both to go to your rooms for bickering please." Again, it's fault-neutral ("you're both for bickering"). If one kid has stopped bickering but the other hasn't, then you'd only ask that kid to go to their room, which reinforces the other for stopping when you asked.

As always, if the kid goes to their room without arguing or complaining about it, you'd tell them they can come out again fairly soon. Once their time is up, you'd want to say, "You're welcome to come out now if you like, but no more bickering please."

I think this is the ideal moment to do some conflict management skills building. After being in their rooms and coming back together again, this is where kids would be more open to your coaching. I think you'll find, however, that most kids, especially older kids, already know what to do. After they've been in their rooms and have settled down, most kids forget all about why they were fighting in the first place.

If bickering happens in the car as it often does, you can still ask them to stop. If they keep at it, now it's time for an if/then statement ("If you keep this up, there won't be any screens later today").

For some kids who bicker more frequently, say multiple times per day, then you can change course after the second or third example of it in the same day. If it happens again, and while the child is still in their room, you can say, "I've had to ask you both a few times today to stop bickering but that doesn't seem to be working. I'd like you to spend more time in your room please so I can make sure it doesn't continue to happen today." In this event, usually about 30 minutes of time in a bedroom is enough for most kids to take you more seriously.

If arguing between kids is just a normal part of what kids do and it's really not a big deal, most kids are perfectly content to move on at this point. You will probably want to move on yourself, especially since you were able to put an end to fighting almost right away and know you can easily do so the next time your kids jockey for power or poke sharp sticks at some chickens.

Takeaways from Chapter 12

- Arguing and bickering between siblings is often a source of upset in families, but it's actually really common and normal for siblings to fight with each other.
- It's also pretty common for siblings to say they hate each other, but in most cases that's not really true and their relationship will often improve as they get older.
- The "just let them work it out" approach rarely works (and often leads to even bigger fights). The "teach them skills to work out their conflict" approach has some merit, but kids are still going to fight because most fights aren't really about anything anyway.
- It rarely helps for parents to try and figure out who started the argument, and most likely both kids have contributed their fair share to the conflict anyway so don't even bother.
- I like using the word "bickering" because it doesn't matter who started it; what matters is that both kids are bickering with each other and that's not okay.
- It's good to ask kids once to stop bickering when it starts, but when that doesn't work what's most effective is to send both kids to their bedrooms for a short while. After a short separation, they'll be motivated to be back in the same room together but to get along better this time to avoid being separated again.

Staying Caught Up on Homework without a Fight

13

Now onto another topic that is a common area of friction in most families who are raising a strong-willed child or teen: endless homework battles.

Every so often in my practice I see that rare kid who just gets their homework done easily and without much prompting or assistance from their parents. Not often, but sometimes. I was blessed in that my three older daughters handled their homework the way I'm guessing you would want your kid to do too:

- When they got home from school, after a snack and some conversation, they started on their homework right away without my saying anything about it.
- They stuck with their homework until it was completed. (They might get distracted a few times but not for very long.)
- Sometimes they'd ask me for help when they got stuck but not very often.
- There was never an expectation that I'd sit next to them while they did their homework.
- They'd put their homework in their backpacks as soon as they finished it and would always turn it in.
- We never once fought about homework, ever.

A dream, right? I'm not sure whether I just lucked into this by having easy-to-parent kids, or whether I somehow established these as my expectations early on so they just got into these habits, or a combination of the two. Either way, I loved it and homework with our older three was a breeze and never a source of conflict in our family. It just got done, almost magically.

DOI: 10.4324/9781003452638-17

I'm certain this is exactly what you want from your own kid, so in this chapter I'm going to tell you everything I know about how to make this happen in your family, or at least as close to it as we can get it.

I mentioned this is how homework went with my three older girls. Daughter number four, however, was a different story altogether. See if any of this sounds familiar. Without involvement from me or my wife, Vicki, she never started her homework on her own. Instead, she'd find anything and everything else to do. Sometimes, she'd eventually get around to starting it, but once she did, she'd put minimal effort into it. She insisted that she didn't understand the assignments, and without our constant help she couldn't possibly get them done. She'd also swear that she'd finished all of her homework but that was rarely true. Unless we stayed on top of it, homework assignments would pile up to the point where she became overwhelmed by the sheer number of them. Every Friday, we would check for missing assignments, and when we learned there were several that she'd not done, she insisted that she had but her teachers must have lost it or not recorded them yet.

So, what was different about her relative to her older sisters? I think in fairness, school was not really her thing. Some kids are just intrinsically self-motivated when it comes to school, and getting good grades probably comes more easily to them. However, this is certainly not the case with every kid, and I really think that's ok. In truth, the only reason I went to school was to see my friends but I was also lucky enough that academics came easily to me. Seeing friends at school wasn't a big draw for our daughter, and honestly, if I had to take a geometry class now, believe me, I'd put up heavy resistance just like her.

Another layer to an oppositional child or teen who may not be keen on academics and school is that this can be a bitter pill for their parents to swallow, especially parents who are well educated and successful. We just naturally expect our kids to be like us, and when they aren't, that can be difficult for a family to navigate. I've seen so many well-intentioned parents who push their kid hard to be like them academically. The problem is that just isn't the kid they have. The kid is probably going to be great at other things in life, but maybe not by way of school and academics. I'd far rather those parents work to have a close, loving relationship with their child, and with some kids you can't have that and also insist they get straight A's that's just the truth of it.

Believe me, I want your child or teen to do their homework just as much as you do. We're still going to have reasonable expectations of them when it comes to school and homework as you'll see, and we're going to get it done without the conflict.

I often tell parents that even if their kid isn't going to college or a trade school right out of high school (the way the parent did or wished they had done), the cool thing about education after high school is that you can pursue it anytime later in life. I also believe that if school and homework aren't a battleground when kids are young, they are far more likely to go to school later in life because they haven't associated school with conflict and bad feelings.

So, again, fully love the kid you have and not the one you wish you had.

Many kids are going to find school more difficult for some very good reasons. Kids with ADHD, a learning disability, problems with executive functioning, and so on are just going to have a harder time with school, homework, and grades. If your child or teen is struggling in school, it's important to rule out other challenges to learning so that you and the school can take steps to better support them or provide additional resources, such as special education services, tutoring, and the like.

However, everything that I'm going to recommend in this chapter is still entirely applicable to kids with attention and/or learning challenges. Even if kids have ADHD or what have you, it's important for them to do their homework and give it a reasonable effort. As I've said before, there are plenty of students with ADHD who still do their homework. This is how the world works anyway; their future selves will still be expected to stay focused at work even when they don't want to. However, one of the problems with diagnoses is that it's fairly common for kids to use that to make the argument as to why expectations for them should be lowered ("You know I can't do homework because I have ADHD, depression, anxiety," etc.). As always, be careful not to lower the bar of expectations to such a degree that kids come to see themselves as less capable than they actually are.

When I say expectations, I don't mean that kids should be expected to get straight as that's just not possible for some no matter how hard they try. What I do mean is that it's reasonable for you to expect that your child or teen keeps up with their homework and puts reasonable effort into it, even if this is harder for them than it might be for someone else.

Learning how to persevere in challenging situations is a great life skill. This is what Angela Duckworth, professor of psychology at the University of Pennsylvania, calls "grit." Grit is the ability to establish and pursue long-term goals that typically require sustained effort and some degree of hardship. Being "gritty" is a predictor of numerous positive traits like resilience, self-control, and self-regulation, along with having a greater probability of being successful in life. Many of the kids I work with are not particularly gritty, especially when it comes to school.

It's also perfectly reasonable to expect that your child or teen will pass their classes, which here in the USA is just getting a D. In my experience, if kids complete most of their homework (and turn it in), they are very likely going to get at least a D and therefore pass their classes. Obviously, very often it might be possible for your kid to do better than a D, but at the very least this should be your minimum expectation and do not waiver from it.

In addition to homework being done and with reasonable effort, I'm going to add two more expectations, both of which seem fair to me.

First, homework should be done as independently as possible. You can help, yes, but you can't do your kid's homework for them. One parent who I worked with told me that she did all of her daughter's homework while she was in high school. I teased her and said that she was the only person I knew who graduated from high school twice. She told me that she did this because "that's the only way she would have graduated from high school." I'm quite skeptical of this. I suspect instead that her daughter worked hard to convince her mom this was the case because she didn't want to do her homework. Truthfully, if I thought my mother would have done all of my homework, I would have gladly let her too.

And, speaking of my mom, when I was in high school, a version of this same scenario did actually play out, or at least partially so. I would ask her to look over my English essays (or she asked to do that, I can't recall), which she started then doing all of the time. "Looking over" turned out to be completely rewriting my essays for me. My mom turned out to be a strong B student in English. For whatever reason, she eventually let go of writing my essays, and as soon as she did my grade shot up to an A. True story.

I'm a great believer that kids should do their homework on their own, or at least as much as possible, especially as they get older. You might still be sitting right next to your kid when they do their homework, and you probably have been doing that for years, so this might take some time and effort to achieve. You'll also never know what your child or teen is actually capable of doing relative to homework if you don't withdraw and test this out. Here's what I advise parents to say to their kids when they'd finally like to mostly step out from homework:

> *I think you're at an age now when most kids start to do their home-work on their own. How cool is that? Here's what I'd like you to do from now on. I'm happy to help you every once in a while when you ask. Maybe a couple of times. Only if you run into something that's par-ticularly hard. But, before you ask for my help, I'd love it if you could first work hard to figure it out on your own, or use other resources like Google or YouTube, or maybe messaging another kid in the class and see if they know the answer. I'll help once or twice, so save me only for the hard stuff and please choose wisely.*

Expect massive protest in response and red herrings galore ("You know I need help with my homework," "I have ADHD so that means you have to help me," and "You don't understand and you're a terrible par-ent for not helping.") A good response to any of these red herrings is "Nonetheless, I have every confidence you'll do great."

In addition to helping your kid develop grit and the ability to work independently, withdrawing from homework sends a clear message that they are the expert on their homework and not you. I'm not particularly good at math so when my daughters hit the fifth grade or so, I told them to count me out when it came to helping them with their math home-work. It's not that I didn't want to; I just knew by then I was not the guy to ask. What I remember saying is "I stink at math. Not only that, I'm not the one sitting in class every day the way you are being taught how to do it. I'd probably do okay if I was, but I've not sat in a math class in some time so you're out of luck."

Do you know how World War I started? I kind of do. Something about a bomb under a carriage. This is my point: kids should be the experts on their own homework. They are in a far better position to know this stuff because they're sitting in class hearing about it, not you. This is an impor-tant message to send your kids, i.e., that it doesn't even make sense that you'd be the person to help them with homework because you're the least qualified person in the room to do so.

Okay, here are our expectations so far: completing most or all home-work assignments, with reasonable effort (not answering just three out of 10 questions), and mostly doing homework on their own.

Here is the final expectation: no tantrums, arguments, or upsets around homework.

In my experience, in most cases, these types of behaviors (like many other negative behaviors) are learned and they serve a very specific function (a purpose). Kids often learn that if they get upset enough, their parents will back off from asking them to do their homework or ask them to put more effort into it "because it's just not worth the fight." Getting you to back off is a highly desirable outcome for a kid (less time doing homework and maybe getting you to do more of it for them), which absolutely reinforces the very behaviors you don't care for (homework upsets). When your kid gets mad and insists that they need your help and then calms down after you give it, your behavior has also been reinforced (negative reinforcement). You got the screaming to stop, sure, and maybe a little more homework done, but it's a fabulous recipe for a kid never persevering on their homework and instead getting mad about it.

This is probably a good time to talk about motivation.

Motivation is just how badly you want something. The "something" in the case of homework might be getting a good grade, the feeling you get when you finish something hard or unappealing, the approval of others, or even just getting parents off your back. The problem here is that for many kids, none of these are strong enough motivators to get the kid to consistently do their homework because often they don't care about any of that.

I've heard many kids say, "I'm just not motivated in school." I don't ever recall a single kid telling me this (or telling their parents) 10 years ago. It's become a thing. I'm not sure where this is coming from, but if I had to guess, it's probably from social media, likely TikTok. This "I'm just not motivated" thing is in the air, so many kids are saying it to their parents and teachers.

I suppose someone could make the argument that something has sapped our kids of their motivation in ways that were not the case with previous generations. Maybe it's uncertainty about the economy, political polarization, or climate change. Who knows? Like the parent who believed her daughter could not graduate from high school unless she did all of her homework for her, I'm skeptical of this as an explanation. Not that these aren't real concerns, but truthfully, I've never had a kid come into my office in a hurry to talk about global warming.

Well, what if they have a mental health condition that is affecting their motivation? This is plausible. For example, we know that depression often makes people less motivated and generally disinterested in doing things, especially things that require a sustained effort. That's fair enough. The problem with this as a causal explanation is that I see plenty of kids who say they're not motivated when it comes to doing their homework but seem highly motivated to do other things, like being on their phones, messaging their friends, or playing video games.

I suspect in many cases the "I'm just not motivated" thing is a red herring, and a pretty good one at that. I could easily see parents being pulled into long (and frustrating) conversations with their kids that probably go like this:

PARENT (P):   Why are you falling so far behind on your homework?
CHILD (C):   I'm just not that motivated to do it.
(P):   What does that mean?
(C):   Why does it matter if I do it?
(P):   Well, it's important to get good grades.
(C):   Not for me.
(P):   Don't you want to go to college?
(C):   No. Bill Gates didn't graduate from college.
(P):   But most people aren't Bill Gates.
(C):   Are you saying you think I can't be Bill Gates?
(P):   No, I'm saying grades are still important.
(C):   That's the only thing that's important to you, my grades. Don't you care about my mental health?
(P):   Of course I do, you know that. But you're failing all your classes.
(C):   That's what I keep trying to tell you but you're not listening. I would do better in school if I was more motivated. *[NOTE: kids will often tell you that you're not listening to them. What they really mean is that you're not agreeing with them.]*
(P):   Well, then what would motivate you?
(C):   Nothing.

This line of argument from a kid also subtly implies that it should be someone else's job to keep them motivated. The kid not doing the work isn't the problem, of course. The problem (or so the argument goes) is that the world has failed to properly motivate them, so, naturally, they're not doing their homework or don't care much about their grades. I suspect, at least in part, why "I'm not motivated" is such a good red herring and why the idea is now firmly imbedded in teen culture and all over socials is that it works. Adults start to believe that they or the educational system are somehow to blame for not properly motivating kids.

There is a version of this same type of red herring that I hear often from parents when they get a report from the teacher that their kid wasn't paying attention in class and was goofing off. The kid's explanation for this is "I'm bored in class." In response, many parents will fully buy into this argument and align with the kid: "Well, he's not being challenged in school so of course he's bored in class. That's the teacher's responsibility." Is it? Or is it the kid's responsibility to still behave in class even if they're bored? I vote the latter.

Here's what's true. It is not your responsibility to help your kid with their motivation problem despite what they might believe. (Well, sort of, but not in the way you might think. We'll get to external motivators in a second.) It's important that you say this out loud to your child or teen and sidestep all the red herrings. What works best when a kid tells you that they're not motivated to do their homework, rather than having endless conversations about it that go nowhere, is just to say, "Well, motivated or not, it's still your responsibility to get all your homework done." A significant life lesson we *all* have to learn is how to do things we don't feel like doing.

Now that we've agreed on expectations, let's see if we can make them happen.

Should You Tell Your Kids When to Start Their Homework?

I think you should but only with really young kids when they first start to get homework. Remember, your goal here is to establish good homework habits that are sustainable through childhood and adolescence.

When younger kids first come home from school, I think it works best to give them 15–30 minutes to decompress, talk about their day (if they want to), and get something to eat. It's not a good idea at all to let your kid have some time on a tablet or watch TV. It's just too hard to pull them off a device and get started on homework. Once settled in after school, you'd want to say, "This probably would be a good time to start your homework." (An ask, not a command, as we discussed earlier in the book.) It's good for young kids to have an established place to do their homework without a lot of distractions (like at the kitchen table). They're probably going to want you to sit next to them because little kids just like being close to their parents, but this is a great time to create a climate of independence and not do so.

Rather than sit next to them, it's better to just be around doing whatever you would normally do. This communicates that homework is their activity and not a joint one, and you can easily walk over to give them help when they ask. It's also good not to walk right over when they have a question because often if you give them a few minutes, they figure out a solution on their own and forget all about you.

If you're starting to get the sense that your child is getting into the habit of asking for your help more than they really need it, you can just say something about that like, "You seem to be asking me for help a lot. I'd like you to spend more time on the problems and because you're a smart kid I'm pretty sure you'll figure it out eventually. How about I help you twice each time you do your homework but only when you're really stuck?" Of course, any time you see them persevering and working hard to solve a problem on their own, make a big deal about it ("Oh my goodness, you super smart kid! I saw how hard you worked hard on that problem. That's a big kid thing to do!").

Let's say they start to struggle and get frustrated by the problem, or maybe they're mad at you for not helping. As I've discussed throughout the book, never talk to or engage with a kid who's speaking to you harshly or in a disrespectful way. In this scenario, if they do, you can say, "I'm happy to help but not if you talk to me that way. Can you ask for my help in a more gentle way please?" If they pull that off, re-engage and, if not, just walk away and don't reengage until they're being nice to you again, no matter how long that takes.

If your child gets up and walks away from their homework, ask them gently to please come back and finish. If they ignore you, say nothing more for now and avoid telling them to come back to the table over and over because that's just a tug-of-war. Don't worry though; we'll still get them to do their homework eventually.

Once kids get older, maybe starting around the ages of seven or eight, the idea of a homework time and location starts to change organically. Kids are often in sports or doing other activities after school, so a specific homework time right after school might not be doable. They're also more mature (hopefully) and have the capacity to do their homework later in the afternoon or early evening.

I also like giving kids, especially teenagers, a lot of latitude as to where they do their homework (like in their bedrooms), as long as they're actually doing it of course. If a kid typically has just a few missing assignments but in general is working hard to stay caught up, doing their homework in their bedrooms is fine even with the obvious distractions. This gives middle schoolers and teenagers a sense of autonomy, which is often something that they crave.

With older kids, I feel strongly that you should never tell them to start their homework. There are several reasons for this, as follows.

As you know, strong-willed kids can be very oppositional when asked to do something. Not wanting to do homework is probably right at the top of their list, so asking them to get started opens the door to a world of problems, most of which can be avoided by simply not asking them. You're very likely going to get into a tug-of-war ("I'd like you to start your homework" followed by "No I don't want to") and countless red herrings ("I don't know how to do it," "Homework is stupid," "I'm too depressed to do it," etc.). Your kid is likely going to start getting worked up and become disrespectful, and although it's best to stay low and slow of course, it becomes too easy to get caught up in an argument.

You never have to ask kids to do their homework each day because it's understood that they won't have access to any devices until it's done (more on leveraging devices shortly). They're free to decide where in their day and evening they'd like to do their homework, which gives kids the opportunity to structure their day and learn time management skills. The message here is "It doesn't matter to me when it gets done, as long as it's done in time for you to wind down before bed." (No doing homework at midnight, that's not practicing good time skills.)

Last, not asking your kid to start their homework clearly communicates that it's their job to be on top of this and not yours. That also sends a corresponding positive message, which is that you have every confidence that they'll get it done and trust their ability to do so.

Leverage

You've probably figured out by now the role that cell phones, tablets, gaming systems, and other screens will play in all of this.

For kids who struggle to get their homework done, all devices and screens should be disabled as soon as they walk in the door. If your kid runs on the more agreeable side, you can make it a rule that all devices go up on the kitchen counter and stay there until you decide they can grab them again. For less agreeable kids who might be unwilling to do this, you can follow the steps I outlined earlier in the book and program your house's router to automatically disable devices at a certain time and use the phone's parental controls or a third-party app to shut off a phone right after school. Kids do not need their phones to do their homework;

this is a myth that they happily will let you believe so they can hang onto their phones.

I do not recommend you ever take a kid's word that they did their homework unless they have a great track record of being honest in this area. Many do not. Before you enable devices, the kid should come to you every day and tell you that they've finished their homework. However, before enabling devices, I highly recommend that you verify work completion. That can be done in a variety of ways, such as asking them to show you a screenshot of the assignment before it's submitted online, or letting you look at a hard copy of any homework completed before it goes in their backpack. What I tell parents to tell their kid is, "If I don't see it, it wasn't done."

Most older kids now use a laptop to do their homework; however, this can make it difficult to monitor whether they're actually doing homework on the device or goofing off. In my area of the USA, many schools issue Chromebooks that are taken home with the student. These school-issued Chromebooks are configured in such a way that they are reasonably well locked down and don't allow access to social media, gaming, and so on. Using one of these Chromebooks is far more preferable than using a personal laptop for this reason.

If your child or teen has to use a personal laptop and they frequently try to do anything other than homework on it, a low-tech solution is just to have them sit at the kitchen table when they do their homework with the screen facing outward so you can glance at what they're doing from time to time. If you keep noticing that they keep misusing the laptop on any given day, just send them away from the table and let them know they can't come back until they're ready to do their homework whenever that is (but the laptop stays, obviously).

Remember, no devices or any other privileges until kids do their homework. If they decide not to do any of their homework that day, let that go and say nothing. However, do not allow them to take their phone to school the next day or earn any device time until their homework is done. It's not a big deal for your kid to skip homework for a day, and most kids will eventually go back to doing it in a day or two.

Periodically Checking in on Missing Assignments

Not all kids are going to need what I'm about to describe as a part of their homework routine, but many will. It's also the part of the homework routine that most parents really dislike, which is understandable because it takes some time and effort. In a perfect world, you wouldn't need to take these extra steps, but for kids who routinely fall behind on their assignments and accumulate quite a few missing assignments, unfortunately it's the only way that I know of to solve the problem.

Currently, just about every school seems to provide parents with a means to log in and see a list of the homework assigned in each class, the due date, and whether or not it's been completed and submitted. It's not a perfect system by any means, but it seems to work pretty well with an exception that we'll discuss shortly. If your kid has a track record of falling behind in their homework completion, you're going to have to make use of this online system.

I don't recommend that you log in every day to see what homework your child or teen still needs to do; that seems like too much work. However, I do recommend that you do so on a weekly basis with Fridays being the day of choice. This just becomes part of the homework routine that your kid will come to expect every Friday. If you find that there are no missing assignments, that's great of course, and you don't need to do anything. That very likely means that the homework routine you've set up is working fine, and along with that your kid is likely now passing their classes.

However, on Fridays, if there are missing assignments, you would want to casually mention that ("Looks like you've got a few assignments to knock out this weekend"), and, obviously, there would be no device time that evening or at any point during the weekend until the missing assignments have been completed and submitted. Not just no device time—nothing else that's fun, like spending time with friends, sleepovers, family outings, and so on. Make maximum use of the Premack Principle: homework first, fun second. And please, as I mentioned earlier in the book, don't ever accept the "deal" that so many kids offer, i.e., that they'll promise to do their homework on Sunday if you let them see their friends on Saturday unless the kid has a history of truly making good on that.

Again, no need to remind them to do their homework on the weekend; they either will or they won't, but as always let the contingencies you've set up do the work for you. No need to argue about it either if they complain ("You know what the rules are around homework. Do it or don't do it, that's up to you.")

If there are just a few missing assignments, that's pretty easy and most kids should be able to knock those out relatively quickly and still enjoy their weekend. However, if you're just beginning to implement your new homework routine and your kid already has many missing assignments, what works best is just to ask them to complete a reasonable amount before you enable devices. They can't possibly complete every single missing assignment all at one time, and they still need the reinforcement to stay motivated.

I can't easily define "reasonable"; that depends on the kid's age, how long they can focus, the difficulty of the assignment, and so on, but you'll know it when you see it. A good ballpark for reasonable is an hour or two of sustained effort that actually results in one or more assignments being completed and submitted (or physically put into a backpack). Again, verify their work before they submit it because many kids will turn in blank assignments online, hoping that you won't catch on. If some homework is done nightly and some on the weekends, most kids can eventually get caught up or at least mostly caught up, thereby raising their grades before the end of the quarter or semester.

All of this becomes easier at the start of the new quarter, semester, or school year because at that time they will have zero missing assignments and they can start fresh. The techniques described in this chapter should help your kid from falling behind again thus requiring less effort from you and them from one week to the next.

The only "flaw" in this system by which you check for missing assignments is that it's really true that teachers can be slow to mark them as submitted in the online system. As I mentioned earlier, kids will capitalize on this weak link in the chain if you let them by telling their parents that they really did the work, but it just hasn't been recorded yet. That's why it's important to look over and verify work completion before assignments are submitted to avoid this problem. If there's still any confusion about what was turned in and what wasn't, you can ask your kid to verify this by emailing their teacher about whether they received the homework and copy you on the message so you can see the response.

A Final Word on All of This from Our Daughter

Vicki and I had to implement every single strategy that I've described in this chapter to get daughter #4 to consistently do her homework and ultimately graduate from high school, which I'm happy to say that she did and on time.

Knowing that this had been a bit of a struggle for her, as I sat down to write this chapter, I asked her if she had any advice that I could include in the book for parents whose kid might be having a hard time doing their homework too. She thought about it for just a second and here's her advice now as an adult looking back: "Um, yeah, tell them not to let their kid use their phone unless all of their homework is done."

And there you have it.

Takeaways from Chapter 13

- Here's what we're aiming for on homework, and it's entirely doable: getting all or most homework completed on time, with little or no help from you (no more sitting next to your kid), and without fighting or arguing about it. A dream come true.
- Not all kids are great students and that's okay. However, almost all kids are capable of staying caught up on their homework and at least passing their classes.
- Doing homework consistently and independently builds grit, an important quality that will take your kid far in life.
- Kids will often say "I'm not motivated in school." This is likely a social media-induced thing that has seeped into teen culture. It's not your job to motivate your kid in school. ("Well, motivated or not, you still need to do your homework.")
- It's good with younger kids to establish a homework time and a place to do it, but with older kids you can let go of both.
- Believe it or not, it works best to never tell your kid to do their homework. Instead, keep all devices and screens off until homework is done and verified by you, no matter how long it takes them to do it.
- It may be necessary every Friday for you to check online and see what assignments are still missing and make it a family rule that nothing fun happens on the weekend (no devices, no friends, and no fun) until all of the homework is done or at least a reasonable amount as defined by you.

Getting Things Done   **14**
Chores and Helping Out Around the House

Not all families ask their kids to do chores and help out around the house, but I highly recommend that you do. Some parents feel like their child or teen's main focus should be on their schoolwork, sports, or other activities. I see the logic in this, but I'm a great believer that kids can do more than one thing at a time and managing a variety of responsibilities, especially as they get older, and doing so is good for them in a number of ways.

Here is the rationale for asking your child or teen to help out around the house, as well as why the next chapter focuses on teens getting their driver's license and a part-time job.

Chores, obtaining a driver's license, and getting a part-time job are responsibilities that were a routine part of growing up and becoming an independent adult in previous generations, but have become far less common among Gen Zs and Gen Alphas. Peter Gray, a research professor of psychology and neuroscience at Boston College, has argued persuasively that one of the contributors to the current mental health epidemic is that parents are now less likely to provide kids with opportunities to engage in independent activities that were common in the past. These opportunities include time playing without adult supervision, taking reasonable, age-appropriate risks (such as walking alone to a park, climbing fences, and so on), contributing to the family (helping out around the house), and taking on what we think of as more adult responsibilities like driving or employment.

Gray's argument is that without giving kids the opportunity to make decisions on their own, learn how to overcome common fears by taking and mastering risks, and parents asking them to take on age-typical responsibilities, we are raising a generation of anxious young people who struggle with making independent decisions, more so than any other time in human history. Research has also shown that kids who do chores

DOI: 10.4324/9781003452638-18

just generally feel better about themselves. For example, Elizabeth White and her colleagues found that children who regularly helped around the house had higher scores on prosocial behavior (positive behavior toward others), greater academic ability, stronger peer relationships, and better overall life satisfaction.

Let's take a look at the data on chores. In a survey conducted by Braun Research of over 1,000 adults in the USA, 82% reported having regular chores growing up, but only 28% said that they require their own children to do them. This matches my experience of the kids I see in my practice: not many of them are doing chores. I also find that some parents would love to have their child or teen do chores, but many of them have given up on that because the kid just refuses to do them.

There are a number of reasons why it's beneficial for kids to do chores. It teaches them that there is value in helping the family and contributing to the overall good of the household. Chores allow kids to get into the habit of working at and sticking with tasks that they find uninteresting and sometimes even unpleasant, which helps them build a strong work ethic. I also believe that doing chores makes kids more considerate roommates in young adulthood, and ultimately better life partners in future relationships. Finally, it teaches them basic life skills that are important for living independently, such as knowing how to clean a bathroom, do dishes, prepare meals, do laundry, take care of pets, and so on.

I feel that the ideal time for kids to start doing chores is when they naturally seem eager and willing to help out, around the ages of three or four. Obviously, not all young kids are eager to please, but in my experience, little kids generally tend to go along with just about anything if their parents think it's a good idea and are backed up by their enthusiasm. It can be small things at that age, such as setting or clearing the table, helping with food prep, picking toys off the floor, and so on. If it's playful and fun, coupled with a lot of praise, most really young kids do quite well with this. It establishes early on that helping out is the thing to do and it's just part of family life. When parents start their kids on chores early, doing chores becomes established as a habit, which lessens pushback in adolescence.

However, if you've waited until your kid is teenager to start asking them to do chores, it's never too late. I've worked with plenty of families who didn't start asking their kids to do chores until late adolescence, with great success.

I'm not a big fan of paying kids to do chores and making their allowances tied to chores. I once worked with a 12-year-old girl, and her parents had a very hard time getting her to help around the house. They started working with a behavior specialist, and the plan they had set up was that the girl earned a certain dollar amount for each chore that she completed. On the surface, that seemed like a sensible enough plan. However, in practice, this got her to do some chores here and there, but she only did them when she wanted some cash, which wasn't very often. The system was also very frustrating for her parents because they were left with any chore that she didn't feel like doing that day, which was most days.

I think this sends the wrong message to kids, i.e., that they only need to help the family when they feel like it and if they're paid to do it. This feels far too transactional for me. (Never mind the fact that it would bug me to have to empty the trash while my kid was in their bedroom having fun.) I think kids should help simply because it's the right thing to do, and part of living in a family means that we sometimes contribute to the greater good even when there's nothing in it for us than just that. Looking at it from this perspective shifts the focus away from kids only paying attention to their own immediate needs, and, instead, focusing on the needs of others and the well-being of the family.

In terms of allowance, what I've found to be far more effective is still giving one to kids but making their allowance a completely separate issue from doing chores. An allowance teaches kids how to budget, how to save, as well as the value of delaying gratification (if they want something that's more expensive, they have to wait and save up their allowance). Chores are just chores—they're part of living in a family.

Speaking of an allowance and learning money management skills, I highly recommend that parents open a teen checking account once kids are old enough. Someone suggested this to me when my daughters were in their early teens and I loved it. The account came with an ATM card, which thrilled my girls to no end because it made them feel very grown up when they used it to go shopping, paying for a meal at a restaurant, and so on.

We agreed in advance what their allowance was to be used for (and what it wasn't, along with a rule of no cash withdrawals) and how much to set aside each month for savings. In general, we established that their allowance was for entertainment, special makeup or hygiene products beyond the basics, and clothing. I would transfer a set amount into their accounts each month, and they were free to do as they liked with it. Their checking accounts were attached to mine, which made it easy for me to see where and how they were spending their money. I was also careful to make the monthly amount a little less than what I thought they actually needed, which put them in a position of having to budget carefully and really think through each purchase. This also took me out of the position of my kids asking for money ("Can I have $20 to go to the movies?"), which I'm sure they appreciated too. If they ran out of money, they'd need to wait until their next transfer rather than me bailing them out.

Again, I believe it's important for kids, no matter what their age, to do some chores on a daily basis, preferably before they engage in fun or recreation. We're back again to the Premack Principle (work before play), but it's actually more than that. You're trying to instill a lifelong value in your kids that we take care of responsibilities and obligations first before we rest and recreate. (Not that we can't sometimes have fun first, we all do that on occasion.)

The daily part of doing chores is important because you're trying to instill a positive habit, something we do almost automatically without thinking about it, and that works better than something done only occasionally (for example, cleaning out the garage).

In my experience, most kids are quite capable of doing at least two or three daily chores as well as one or two more time-consuming weekly chores, typically done on the weekend. Depending on age, a daily chore might be something like emptying the trash, feeding, walking, or cleaning up after a dog, a quick room pickup, emptying the dishwasher, and the like. A weekend chore might be deep cleaning the bathroom, mowing the lawn, doing laundry, a real room cleanup, and so on. Older teens can make dinner for family once or twice a week or do the grocery shopping.

One of my happiest days as a parent was when I could pass over the responsibility of grocery shopping to my daughters. I really hate grocery shopping and I always have. After each girl got their driver's license, they became the next in line to take over the shopping. Once they got the hang of it, all I'd have to do is hand them the grocery list and off they'd go, and when they returned home, they'd put everything away. It was heavenly.

Please don't sell your kids short on chores. I treated a family who had a 17-year-old daughter who had just graduated from high school. She had *just one chore*: emptying the dishwasher every day. That's it, and she never even did that without being told to and always with a fuss. ("Why is this my job? This is stupid.") I asked her parents why they had this able-bodied human living in the house, but they never asked her to help more. Yet the idea seemed foreign to them. To make it even more puzzling, as far as I could tell, this girl had nothing but time on her hands because she wasn't working or going to school. (We fixed all of this.)

In truth, the girl's parents never asked her to do more because she very effectively trained them out of doing so. She would give them so much grief when she emptied the dishwasher that they didn't dream of asking her to do anything else just to avoid further conflict. That was obviously the function of her complaining as it very effectively got her out of doing more chores. Her parents, unintentionally of course, reinforced her over and over again for complaining, with the end product being a kid who did almost nothing around the house. Sadly, it also created a sense of strong entitlement in her and sent her the message that nobody thought she was capable of anything more.

Speaking of entitlement and selling kids short, when I was growing up we were fortunate enough to have a swimming pool. One day while I was in high school, I had a friend over and he casually asked me how often my parents asked my brothers and me to clean the pool. I sheepishly told him that they paid to have a guy come to clean it every week, and he said, "What? How many brothers do you have? Your parents *pay* to have someone else to do it?!" Embarrassing to say the least. He was totally right; of course, my brothers and I should have been asked to clean the pool and probably a lot more than that too.

Okay, I think we've established all of the benefits that come from asking kids to help out, but it's not as easy as just asking, is it?

If you're reading this, I bet you want your child or teen to help out more around the house and do their chores consistently, but I'm guessing it's a battle. They probably argue and complain about their chores, put you in a position of asking them over and over to do them (nagging), and even if they finally get started on the chore, I bet sometimes they do it poorly. Worse still, maybe they just refuse to do the chore altogether, so you've given up and you just do it yourself. As I said, the function (purpose) of all of those behaviors is to make it so miserable for you that you back off and ask less or hope that you'll decide the battle isn't worth it and do everything yourself. Of course, if you end up doing the chore yourself, that just teaches the kid to argue even more because they know you'll eventually cave.

Let's change all of that. Here's what you're aiming for: your kids to do a few daily chores and weekly chores, to do them when they're first asked (or maybe with a second prompt as we'll see in a minute but no more than that), and to do the job reasonably well, all with a minimum of arguing or even better, no arguing at all.

I bet we can hit that mark.

I'm going to offer you two alternatives, and then you can pick the one that you think is best suited to your particular kid.

The first plan is geared more toward kids who don't resist chores as much. They will mostly do their chores when asked, but not necessarily within the time frame that you prefer. This type of kid generally means well, but rarely does their chores without being asked or frequently forgets to do them until you remind them. I find this plan works for many kids, but if it doesn't, you can always go to the second plan.

The second plan is for kids who are more oppositional and strong-willed. It's not so much that they forget to do their chores and need the reminder; it's more that they simply refuse to do them when you ask them to.

Two Step-By-Step Plans for Getting Chores Done Peacefully

Plan One (For Less Resistant Kids)

As I said this first plan is for more agreeable and less resistant kids, it's the plan I used with my own four daughters and it never failed me.

For these more agreeable kids, it's not so much that they object to doing their chores. They mostly do them and do them reasonably well. However, they need frequent reminders to do their chores; otherwise they'd rarely or never get them done. These reminders often become a source of irritation because parents feel they shouldn't have to ask their kid over and over to do their chores, and I completely agree. This plan solves that problem.

Set Timelines and Use Mitigated Speech

I find it best when a chore needs to be done that it works best and reduces conflict if you do not ask your kid to do it immediately, especially with teenagers. Some chores, obviously, need to be done right away, like emptying the dishwasher because you need to put more dishes into it right then, but the vast majority of chores do not. Whether someone empties the trash now or an hour from now really doesn't matter all that much. Similarly, a room can be picked up almost anytime; there's usually no urgency to it.

As we discussed earlier, teenagers have reached an age in which they are very sensitive to power imbalances and not losing face in the same way that adults are. This ties into the concept of asking not commanding that I talked about earlier in the book, i.e., using what's known as mitigated speech to phrasing things in a way that sounds more like an ask rather than an order. No one responds well to an order, kids included. When you ask someone to do something right away, especially if it's phrased like a command, it substantially increases the probability that you'll get resistance. Phrasing something in a way that sounds more like an ask (even though it really isn't an ask) often makes a kid more likely to do it and in an agreeable way.

Rather than asking for a chore to be done immediately, I find it works far better to give kids a time frame by which you'd like it done because doing so gives them the freedom and autonomy of deciding where in their day they'd like to fit it in. Adults have this same freedom (most of the time, anyway), and teenagers value that just as much as we do.

I find with chores, both daily and weekly chores, it works best to establish in advance a time by which you'd like the chores to be done. For example, you might decide that you'd like your child or teen to have all of their daily chores completed before you sit down to dinner, or maybe all of their longer weekend chores done by noon on Saturday. You don't really care when they do the chore so long as it's done, and this gives kids more of a say so in their lives. In addition, if you adopt this approach, you're giving your kid an opportunity to practice building their time management skills (what needs to be done and by when). It's just a part of life that people learn how to structure their days in order to meet whatever obligations are in front of them.

Once the chores themselves have been assigned and you've agreed to a time they need to be completed by, there is no reason for you to remind your kids to get their chores done before the deadline. Resist the temptation to do so please as they'll just get annoyed with you, and rightfully so because they haven't hit their deadline yet. Just act as if you have every confidence your kid will get everything done in time, even if they might not.

What to Say When the Deadline Isn't Met

Expect that your kid will routinely miss the established deadline, my daughters did too. This is normal and perfectly okay so don't get worked up about it. There are a lot of reasons for kids missing a chore deadline, such as simply forgetting to do it (like we all do sometimes), getting caught up in something and losing track of time, or, of course, the obvious one: they just didn't feel like doing it.

Now it's time for a prompt. This is where it's really important to be matter-of-fact and not be angry or accusatory. If you've established in advance that a daily chore needs to be done by the time you sit down to dinner and you know it hasn't, then it's time to say, "Hey I don't think you got to the dishwasher. Go ahead and take care of that now please before you sit down." Or let's say it's noon on Saturday and nothing has been done, you'd want to say, "Hey it's noon already. I'd like you to get started on your chores now please."

You'll notice that this prompt includes the word now. They've missed the deadline either out of forgetfulness or whatever, so it's important that it be done now. At this point, many kids will be apologetic and say something like, "Oh I'm sorry, I forgot" (true or not, it doesn't matter). A gentle, easy response to that is, "Oh no problem. Thanks for taking care of that." As long as they do it right then agreeably, that's what counts.

However, let's say the kid digs in at this point and refuses to do the chore. You've come this far in the book so I'm hoping you already know the answer. Time to leverage devices by using pause, earn, and return ("I'm going to shut off your phone until it's done") or use an if/then statement ("If you expect to be on your devices tonight, then you're going to need to get your chore done please").

As I said, a lot of kids respond to this plan really well. If you don't get a lot of pushback, chores are typically done reasonably well, and if your child or teen doesn't flat out refuse to do the chore altogether, this plan should be all you need. It's very gentle, collaborative, and requires just a single reminder from you so there won't be a need to nag your kid over chores.

Plan Two: For More Resistant Kids

This is the strategy that you'd want to adopt if you'd tried Plan One without success, or you've got a kid who fights you on everything and you're reasonably sure Plan One would be a bust. This would be the plan I'd recommend for kids who routinely refuse to do their chores, and even if you can finally get them to do the chore, it's done poorly. You'll probably notice this plan has a lot of similarities to how to get these kids to do their homework, so if you've mastered that this should be a breeze for you.

Make Use of the Premack Principle Again

Again, as we've talked about many times in this book, responsibilities come before fun and recreation.

If your child or teen struggles with doing chores, then you'll want to make use of the Premack Principle here as well. Chores should be done first; privileges like screens come second. For these more resistant kids, I recommend that screens are routinely off and inaccessible after school or first thing on the weekends and then are only enabled once your kid has done all their chores and done reasonably well.

I've seen a lot of families do the reverse: the kid still has their phone before they've done their chores, or they'll be allowed to game for a while before they are supposed to start their chores. This might work just fine with easier kids who mostly follow the rules, but it absolutely does not work with more oppositional kids. I'm sure you've tried pulling your kid off their gaming system to do their chores, so you know it's nearly impossible.

Chores first, always.

Leveraging

As was the case with homework, there's really no reason to ask a kid each day to start their chores. Doing so would probably just annoy them and invite a less-than-ideal response ("Why should I?"). It's just understood that chores need to be done before their devices are enabled. Again, say nothing and just wait. At some point, your kid is going to ask if they can get on their phone, tablet, gaming system, or what have you. If it's on a weekend, they'll want those things too, but they might also want permission to see a friend, go on an outing, and so on. When they ask, the best response is: "Sure, I'd be happy to turn on your phone (take you to your friend's house, etc.) but I think you know what needs to be done first, yeah?"

At that point, you've got pretty good leverage, and there's a good chance they'll get started on their chores. If not, then go back to waiting. Essentially, what you're communicating is that you won't back down from your expectation that the chores need to be done, nor will you fight about it or try to talk them into it. ("Do it or don't do it, that's up to you, but nothing happens until it's done.")

Here's a playful alternative to when your kid just looks at you and says, "I'm not doing my chore." It doesn't always work (but I guess nothing always works when you get right down to it) but it's worth trying. This tends to work the best when you've been following the steps outlined in this chapter for a while, and most of the time your kid has started doing their chores without a fight. Every kid has a bad day, and every kid gets stubborn sometimes. When they tell you they're not going to do their chore, you can try saying this somewhat playfully but not sarcastically:

> *"No? You're not going to do it. Well, shoot, Alright, I guess that's how it is. Wait though, what do you think I'm going to say next; do you know?"* (And then the kid will probably say,) *"You're not going to let me have my phone until I do!"* (And then you can say,) *"Yeah, that's true, you're right. How about we just skip over all that and maybe you just get it done? Or not, I'll let you decide."*

Then, just walk away and see what happens.

We're also going to need to address what tends to be common with strong-willed and oppositional kids as well, which is doing their chores poorly. They just don't put much effort into it, or only do part of the chore. I think the easiest workaround to this is always do a quick check of their chores before you agree to enable devices. You can just make this part of the chore routine and ask that your child or teen call you to take a quick look at what they've done before moving on to something else. If they did a great job, heap on the praise.

If something isn't done to your liking (within reason—kids aren't per-fect, so a little flexibility here is good), then just matter-of-factly point out what you'd like them to do differently and then walk away until they call you back again. If your kid keeps calling you but it's clear that they know how to do it and they just aren't, it's best to say this:

> *"Look, I think you know what needs to be done so I'm not going to keep coming back here again and again. The next time you call me please, I'd like you to do it correctly. If not, I think we're done for today and you can try again tomorrow, but no devices until then."*

Typically, once all components of this strategy are implemented, it will take at least a few weeks or even a few months before chores start to go more smoothly. However, once your own behaviors around chores have changed and you've established a new routine, most kids will eventually come around because they'll learn that there's just nothing in it for them to keep fighting you on it. You will have removed all of the inadvertent reinforcement for your child or teen to avoid doing their chores (like the girl who complained every day about emptying the dishwasher) and replaced that unhelpful reinforcement with reasonably effective incentives to get their chores done, and hopefully peacefully at that.

Paul Versus Timmy

I'm going to end this chapter with a story. It's about me and it's a little embarrassing because I did all the wrong things in an attempt to get a kid to do a chore, so don't do any of this.

In the very first residential program for young boys where I worked, while I was still very new at the job, I was in the facility alone one day with a super cute seven-year-old boy named Timmy. Timmy and I were still trying to figure each other out, but as you'll see he was way ahead of me in that department.

He was home that day because he refused to go to school, and my boss gave me the task of making sure Timmy cleaned his room. One of the rules in the facility was that the boys needed to fold all of the clothes in their dresser. In hindsight, it was a dumb rule because, really, why does that matter to anyone? (There are a LOT of rules in residential treatment programs and most of them don't make any sense.)

I was young and invested in the rules so when I sent Timmy down to his room I reminded him to make sure he folded the clothes in his dresser. "Okay, Paul." No pushback, whatsoever. This was something I knew he could do because he'd done it many times. About 10 minutes later, Timmy called me to his room and said that he was finished. He did a pretty good job on the room itself but when I looked in his dresser, everything was all balled up and most definitely not folded.

I reminded him again to fold his clothes and that I would be back, and he said, "Okay Paul." He called me back again and still his clothes weren't folded. I'm ashamed to say that this went on for some time—I probably got called down there six or seven times, and by then Timmy was clearly enjoying himself. I, however, was not. I finally got angry and yelled, "TIMMY! Don't call me down here again until you do it right!"

So not the thing to do. Timmy was clearly playing a game of tug-of-war with me, and I didn't even know that I was in the game, much less what to do about it.

This time I stomped off; only he followed me out of his room. In the hallway, just sitting there, was an industrial-sized bucket full of water, which he picked up and dumped all over my feet.

Final score: Timmy 1, Paul 0.

If you're wondering if I ever got Timmy to fold his clothes that day the answer is no. I just didn't know how but today, of course, I'd do it much differently. And since you've made it to the end of this chapter, I bet you'd have a pretty good idea of how to get Timmy to fold those clothes. Just plan something you know he wants to do, like play a game of basketball or go to the park, and let him know you'd be happy to take him whenever he finishes folding his clothes. Alternatively, if it wasn't practical to plan some high interest activity, it would have also worked just to let him know that he was welcome to come out of his room as soon as his clothes were folded properly. If he takes forever to fold them that's okay, but guaranteed he's going to want to get it done.

Takeaways from Chapter 14

- Chores are often a significant source of conflict in families, but they don't have to be. You can get your strong-willed and oppositional child or teen to do their chores peacefully, without asking them more than once.
- Kids who do chores are happier and better adjusted. It helps them be more independent, teaches them the value of focusing less on themselves and more on others, and develops valuable life skills.
- I generally don't like tying an allowance to chores or paying kids to do them. That just seems too transactional. It's better to ask kids to do chores because that's just part of living in a family.
- It's most effective to create a culture within your family that doing daily and weekly chores always comes before fun, such as being on a device or gaming system or seeing friends.
- For some less resistant kids, rather than asking them to do chores right away, it's more effective to set an agreed-upon time each day by which they should be done, such as "I'd like you to have all your chores done by the time we sit down to dinner every night please." If the chores aren't done by the deadline, you can give one matter-of-fact reminder (and only one, no badgering).
- For kids who are more resistant to doing chores or maybe even refuse to do them altogether, rather than setting an agreed-upon time frame for their completion, it is more effective to keep devices off each day and only enable them after chores are completed (and looked over by you).

Bigger Kid Stuff

15

Overcoming Reluctance to Getting a Driver's License and a Part-Time Job

I'm going to continue down the path we embarked on in the last chapter in which I made the argument that one of the contributors to the child-hood mental health epidemic is the lack of opportunities for Gen Z and Gen Alpha to develop age-appropriate independence. This idea was pro-posed by Peter Gray, a researcher at Boston College. Just as fewer teens are helping out around the house in comparison with previous gener-ations, it's also true that it's become less common for kids to get their driver's license and a part-time job.

Here's what the data tell us. According to the Federal Highway Association, in 1983, a little under half (46.2%) of 16-year-olds had their driver's license. However, by 2018, that number dropped down to only 25.6%. In fact, in 2018, only 60.9% of 18-year-olds had their driver's license. Currently, teenagers are even less likely to have a part-time job according to the Bureau of Labor Statistics. Among kids between the ages of 16 and 19 in the USA, the percentage who had part-time jobs has dropped from a high of 31% in 1998 to just 17.6% in 2020.

Not to point fingers, but I think parents are playing a role in this. Relative to previous generations, I don't think parents currently are as inclined to routinely ask their teenagers to get their license and hold down a job. I'm sure this comes from a caring place (not wanting to push their kid into something they believe they might not be ready for), but I don't think this does kids any favors and actually slows down the process of them growing up and maturing.

As I've said in the previous chapters, I'm a strong proponent of parents not giving kids a pass on age-typical responsibilities because the mes-sage you're sending is that you believe they're not capable of navigating challenging situations. If you believe that, I promise you they're going to believe it too. For kids to build resilience and become self-confident, it's really important that you ask them to do harder things, especially things

DOI: 10.4324/9781003452638-19

that are very likely within their reach with your help and support (and maybe some nudging).

However, what do you do when you've got a oppositional kid who's reluctant to do harder things? Or, I suppose, any kid for that matter who just doesn't want to get their driver's license or a job? I believe for the vast majority of kids you can make this happen, and in this chapter, I'll outline the strategies that my colleagues and I implement every day with great success.

Steps for Helping Reluctant Kids to Get Their Driver's License

Every so often in my practice, I see a 16-year-kid who's eager to get their driver's license, but in most cases they're highly reluctant to do so.

The most common argument I hear a kid make is that they're too anxious to drive. Relative to previous generations, Gen Z does report experiencing more anxiety. It's also become more common for today's parents to accept this argument and let their kids delay the process of acquiring their driver's license. There is also an element of what psychologists call "social proof," i.e., kids see their friends also not getting their licenses, which then normalizes not doing so. Parents also see other parents not pushing their own kids to drive, which normalizes it further.

There exists a sound rationale for asking kids to pursue their driver's license despite the cultural shift away from doing so. First, we know that the way to become less anxious about something isn't by avoiding it. That actually makes the anxiety worse in the long run even though in the short run avoidance brings some momentary relief. Second, again, it sends the wrong message: if something makes you nervous, just don't do it.

Research tells us that the treatment for anxiety is opposite action— stepping into scary situations on purpose (exposure) because with practice the scary situation stops being so scary. The first time someone puts themselves into a situation that makes them uncomfortable, such as going to a party where they don't know anyone, speaking in public, or, in this case driving a car, the person's anxiety level will be at its highest. This is also the point in which someone's urge to avoid or escape the situation also will be at its highest, which is why both kids and adults gear up to try something scary for the first time but then bail right before doing it. People also often mistakenly believe that their anxiety will just continue to get worse and worse, to spin out of control, but this isn't the case.

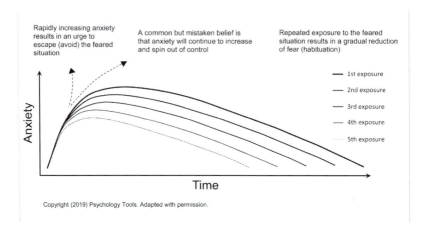

Copyright (2019) Psychology Tools. Adapted with permission.

Figure 15.1 The Anxiety Reduction Curve

Figure 15.1 shows how anxiety gradually reduces with each exposure to the feared situation.

It can be really helpful to explain all of this to kids so they understand that each time they do the scary thing it becomes less and less scary. Some kids won't agree with this and insist it doesn't work that way with them, but thankfully it will.

As parents, the life lesson we're trying to teach our kids is this: doing hard things makes us stronger, builds grit, and ultimately makes us less anxious and more resilient human beings. Third, "anxiety" and feeling "nervous" aren't the same thing. Learning how to drive, like any new challenge, brings with it a certain degree of feeling nervous, which is both normal and understandable.

In my practice, I often encourage parents to normalize their use of language with their kids. "Therapy speak" has made its way into popular culture in a way that it often works against children and teens. Parents can "de-energize" conversations (maybe that's therapy speak too) about driving by just being mindful of language. For example, if a kid says, "The thought of driving makes me really anxious," it can be really helpful to respond by saying something like, "Yeah, most people are nervous at first, but once you get the hang of it that goes away." This shift in language alone might not be enough for your kid to agree to drive, but it both normalizes the experience and it's also 100% true.

If you want your kid to be more willing to face their fears and take on new challenges, you need to be careful not to accidentally reinforce their efforts at avoidance. If you accept your teen's argument that they can't learn how to drive because they're "too anxious" and you let them off the hook from driving, that will clearly reinforce more avoidant behavior. Remember, what gets reinforced gets repeated.

Here's another truth in all of this. Kids don't generally know much about why avoidance works against them; they just know they're feeling nervous and would rather not do something that makes them even more nervous. Their attempts to avoid, therefore, make sense if you stand in their shoes. It's obviously good to give our kids a say in things as often as we reasonably can, but sometimes as a parent you just must insist that they do something that will help them even if they don't see it the same way. For example, if your teenager told you that they've decided to drop out of high school because they'd rather play video games all day, you'd just say no to that because you clearly understand it wouldn't be good for them.

Someone reading this might really believe that some kids are just too anxious to drive. I suppose this could be true, but the problem is I've never met one. I've worked with many clinically anxious kids, but all of them ultimately got their driver's license.

The second most common reason I hear from kids as to why they don't want to get their driver's license is, "Why? My parents drive me everywhere." There is a lot of sense to this, of course, and if I had someone ready and willing to meet all of my transportation needs, I doubt I'd want to drive very much either. I don't think anyone would give up this arrangement willingly, so it's obviously up to parents to decide when they're done being their kid's chauffer.

Sometimes, parents will tell me that they're hesitant to allow their teen to drive even if the kid is in favor of it. Maybe the kid is impulsive and doesn't always show the best judgment, or the thought of an ADHD teenager driving safely on the road is hard for them to picture. Here's the cool thing about a kid learning how to drive and ultimately getting their license: it takes a long time for them to do so. From the time they first start driver's education (which where I live is mostly done online) to passing the behind-the-wheel test, there are so many steps along the way with many months in between. The kid has to complete driver's ed; take and pass their written permit test; accumulate enough time behind the wheel with their parents learning how to drive; and finally pass the driving test. There are so many places a parent can slow down the process or put a pause in place if they feel their kid needs more time to acquire the skills or the necessary level of maturity before actually getting their license.

I think the other cool thing about a kid learning how to drive is that it can be a great opportunity for parents and teens to bond over a rite of passage. It can be such a great moment to sit with your teen when they start the car for the first time and slowly creep forward in an empty parking lot or on a road.

When I learned how to drive, I spent the majority of my time in the car with my stepfather, who was by far not the gentlest or most patient of human beings (to say the least). I thought it was going to be a horrible experience, but as it turns out, some of my best childhood memories of him were when he taught me how to drive. He was shockingly relaxed and easygoing about it. I'd make some mistake and thought for sure that he'd be all over me but instead he'd say, "That's okay Paul, it just takes time and practice." (Who is this man, and what have you done with my step-father!)

Normalizing the Expectation

As you might guess, the process begins with not taking no for an answer. If your kid has already voiced reluctance about driving, or maybe you've been letting them off the hook for a while and now you've changed your mind, just know you'll get pushback when you bring the subject up. Expect a ton of red herrings, such as "I told you I was too anxious to drive, why are you forcing me?"; "I'm afraid I'll cause an accident"; or "None of my friends drive either."

As I've talked about throughout the book, when a kid throws out a bunch of red herrings, the worst thing you can do is respond to them as that will just take you down a path that goes nowhere. In addition, as we've also talked about, let go of trying to talk them into getting their license because most kids will just swat away every reason one by one that their parents give them for why they should get it. If you haven't persuaded them to by now, you probably never will. Of course, a little bit of persuading and offering a rationale for driving is fine, but it will become clear to you when to change the direction of the conversation because it will feel like you're trying to persuade a dining-room table.

The conversation might flow like this:

PARENT (P): Hey, let's talk again about the possibility of you getting your driver's license.

CHILD (C): Why? I told you I don't want to.

(P): I know, but I think it's time, yeah?

(C): I'm too anxious, you know that. *[A clear red herring]*

(P): Most people are nervous when they start but that gets better with practice.

(C):	That doesn't work with me. *[Another red herring]*
(P):	I'm confident that you'll do just fine.
(C):	I'm not going to do it. You can't make me.
(P):	Well, I'm not going to argue or get into a long back and forth about it. You may not agree but it's important that you do it anyway. We'll go slowly. The first step will be starting on driver's ed and I'll get that set up for you. Thanks, I appreciate you listening.

That should pretty much be the end of the conversation, and at that point, it's best to just walk away. If you linger, you'll just get more protests and a never-ending stream of red herrings. As I've said before, walking away signals that the conversation is over, and please resist the temptation to respond to more protests or do any more persuading. As is often the case, of course, just telling your kid to begin driver's ed does not mean they're going to do it.

Leverage

The online driver's education course is by far not any teenager's preferred way of passing the time. I don't think the course is super challenging because every kid eventually completes it. How quickly they get through it varies quite a bit, but I've found that the typical range is somewhere between a single weekend and a few weeks depending on how much effort the kid puts into it.

Once you set it up for them online, just start by asking your teen to begin working on it a little bit every day until the course is completed. If this works and your kid seems to be making reasonable progress, you won't need to do anything else and just wait for them to finish.

However, if after a week or so it becomes clear that your kid has put very little effort into it (or maybe even not started it at all), it's time to leverage devices as follows:

PARENT (P):	I see that you haven't done much work on driver's ed. What's that about?
CHILD (C):	*[Prepare for red herrings: "I don't how to log in"; "I thought you wanted me to work on my homework?"; "I forgot"; or "I told you I wasn't doing it."]*
(P):	Hmmm. What should we do about that?
(C):	I don't know.

(P):	Well, how do I normally handle it when I ask you to do something and you don't do it?
(C):	I don't know.
(P):	I kinda think you do. Take a moment.
(C):	So, you're going to take my phone?
(P):	That's right. But, how about this? I'll give you another week or so to start doing it on your own but if that doesn't happen then from now on all devices will be off until you've spent some time working on it each day, say an hour, and with some kind of noticeable progress. And, no seeing friends on the weekend until you've done the hour. Does that seem reasonable?
(C):	No. That's not reasonable at all.
(P):	May I point something out to you?
(C):	No. Okay, what?
(P):	I know you don't like it when you lose your phone, I get that. But you do have a say in all of this, more so than I think you realize. You could do what I ask and then keep your phone all the time. Or not, I suppose. You'll either do your driver's ed or you won't. I'll let you decide.

Then, sit back and wait a week and see what happens. If the kid does it, great. If not, do exactly what you said you were going to do; turn off all devices and restrict contact with friends until they work on driver's ed each day. As was the case with homework and chores, no need to remind your teen each day to do their driver's ed because that will just annoy them. Let your kid come to you every day to say that they did it and verify work completion before enabling devices. It's totally fine if some days they don't work on driver's ed at all, no need to mention it, and then just see what happens the next day and the day after that, but no devices or friends.

You can follow this same strategy throughout the entire process of actually getting the license. Let's say the kid finishes driver's ed but when they go to take the written test, they don't pass it. You'll want to let them try again, of course, but if they still don't pass it a second time it's obvious that they need to study more for the test, maybe with your help but not necessarily. If your kid refuses to study, it's the same procedure, i.e., devices off until they spend a reasonable amount of studying each day. What if they pass the written test but refuse to do the practice driving? Same thing, no devices or friends unless they go driving with you when you offer it.

Here's one final tip on the practice driving that I learned from some-one else. I did it with my own girls and it worked really well. What you don't want is conflict in the car, or your kid arguing with you every single time you try to correct some part of their driving. Before you take them out the very first time, you say some version of this playfully:

> Okay here's how all of this works. I'm the teacher and you are the stu-dent. I'm going to be telling you all kinds of things to do and it works best just to say 'okay.' As you become a better driver, you're going to be tempted to disagree with me from time to time. But, when a teacher tells a student something, they really just want to the student to say 'okay.' Not why or how come, or you're wrong I did turn my signal on in time to change lanes. Just 'okay.' Agreed?

One of my daughters had a bad habit when she first started to drive in that she would drive too far to the right on any given road. I think she did this because oncoming cars made her nervous, understand-ably, so she'd overcorrect and hug the right-hand side of the road. I can't tell you how many times I said to her, "Too far to the right." It became like a mantra or something. One day, when she was really close to getting her license, she did it again and I said, "Too far to the right." This time, she got really mad at me and said, "Dad, why do you keep telling me that!?" We drove another half-mile or so, and this time she was so far to the right that her right tires went off the asphalt and onto the shoulder of the road, causing her to momentarily lose control until she corrected it. She looked over at me as I was smiling and she said, "Don't even say it!"

Steps for Helping Reluctant Kids Get a Part-Time Job

As is the case with learning how to drive, there are countless reasons why it's good for teens to get a part-time job.

Having the ability to get and hold onto a job brings with it all kinds of really great life skills. It teaches kids how to show up somewhere, be on time, even when they don't feel like it, how to interact with customers and coworkers who probably aren't going to be nearly as nice to them as their parents, how to do crummy jobs but still be expected to do them well, how to accept criticism, both fair and unfair, from supervisors barely older than themselves, and so much more.

These are all skills that most people can only acquire by doing, and it's a great way to help kids accelerate their growth and maturity. Teenagers who work just seem more grown up and responsible to me, and probably to their teachers and friends as well. Last, we all want our kids to be independent and self-sufficient someday, and anyone working full-time even at minimum wage is likely going to at least have a roof over their head and food on the table.

Some parents are reluctant to ask their kids to get a part-time job because they feel that their kid isn't able to focus on getting their homework done and working at the same time. I agree with this argument but only if the kid already has a lot of other things on their plate, for example, if they play sports. If not, it seems to me that most kids have plenty of time on their hands and fill it by being online in their bedrooms. An additional benefit of working is that it counteracts the crowding-out effect of devices, i.e., the tendency to spend so much time on a device that it leaves little time for activities that are good for a kid's mental health. I think most kids can focus on both doing their homework and holding down a job, and it's a reasonable expectation that kids be able to do more than one thing at a time.

Some kids are all over this and are motivated intrinsically to start looking for work with little or no parental nudging, and in that case, the process goes smoothly. I once worked with a super anxious-avoidant kid who barely left the house, but one day out of the blue when he turned 15, he told his parents that he wanted to get a job ("You do?"). It was like a miracle and completely unexpected, the opposite in fact of what I would have predicted. And, not 15 and a half, just 15, so no one thought it was even possible but, wow, he was on it. He ended up applying for a job in a fast-food restaurant and was hired by the owner who didn't mind his age.

However, obviously, not all kids are crazy about the idea of getting a job, so I'll walk you through the steps of making this happen.

As is the case with getting a driver's license, some kids just refuse to get a job. Alternatively, they might agree to start looking for a job, but then not actually do it. Again, from the kid's perspective, their reluctance makes sense because who wouldn't rather play video games than work at McDonald's? In addition, for some kids who are more introverted or socially uncomfortable, the thought of working makes them anxious (nervous), so their inclination is to avoid work altogether.

The strategy for overcoming reluctance is exactly as I outlined it for helping kids get their driver's license. You start by normalizing the expectation ("You're at an age when kids get part-time jobs and it's time for you to get one too"), and sidestep any of the predictable red herrings they might throw at you ("You know I don't like being around other people"). Rather than argue or debate it, it's best to express optimism in their ability to get and hold a job ("I'm confident you'll do great with it").

Here are some of the things that I've learned about teenagers and part-time jobs. The first one is always the hardest to get because obviously most kids don't have much in the way of a work history, so that understandably makes a prospective employer nervous. Anything on a resume or job application is better than nothing at all, so even volunteer work improves the kid's chances of getting hired somewhere.

Often the easiest way to get a first-time job is to know someone who can help them get the job, like a friend or a relative. However, I've seen many kids with absolutely no work experience get hired, usually within a few months of looking. Most teens also benefit from their parents' help when it comes to filling out applications just to make sure the kid is presenting themselves as favorably as possible, everything is spelled right, and so on.

The key is to submit a lot of online applications and not be super selective about where they work, at least not for their very first job. It's been my experience that if a kid submits two or three applications a day, every day, they are very likely going to get an interview within a few weeks. (I once had a kid tell their parents that they weren't getting any interviews because apparently there was a "hiring freeze" everywhere. Who knew that periodically all employers got together and made these types of hiring decisions?) Even if it takes a while to get an interview, there's still a value in learning how to submit applications and sticking with the process. In addition, even if a kid gets an interview but doesn't get the job, there's a value in practicing how to interview well.

There are countless teaching moments in helping kids get their first part-time job. Conversations about what employers are looking for in an employee and how to present oneself favorably in an interview, such as what to wear and how to answer common interview questions. Doing practice interviews with kids is really fun and a great way to reduce their anxiety. It's a bit old fashioned to physically go into places and turn in a resume, but there's a skill set that comes with this, which is worth learning and many smaller employers still prefer it.

Okay, so how do you get your kid to apply for jobs?

Leverage

You guessed it! Again, it's the same strategy I've presented on homework, a driver's license, and now employment.

You'd begin by just asking your teen to start submitting two or three job applications a day, either online or in person, every day. Next, give them a week to do so and see what happens. However, if after a week it becomes clear to you that they aren't submitting a few applications each day, it's time to circle back and follow the same script used earlier. Let your kid know that if they don't get moving on it, the next thing that will happen is no devices or friends until they're submitting the requisite number of applications each day.

As was the case with homework, it may not be a good idea that you just take your kid's word for it that they're actually submitting the applications, especially if after a few weeks they've not been called in for an interview. If that is the case, it's helpful to ask them for verification of applications submitted. In most cases, when applying online, the person will receive an email confirmation that the application has been received, which is an easy thing to ask your kid to show to you. On occasion, I've seen some kids submit applications and get called in for interviews, but then just not go to the interview ("I forgot."). You can easily leverage devices and time with friends here too by just asking the kid, "What consequence do you feel is appropriate (loss of devices and not seeing friends) if you bail on an interview again?"

Last, and again it's not very common, some kids will get all the way through this process and actually get hired, but then quit the job impulsively. Not all jobs are right for everyone, obviously, but in this case it works best for the kid to go right back to submitting applications. If this becomes a pattern and you suspect your teen is just "mad quitting" over and over so as to avoid working, you can call them out on this (matter-of-factly, as always) and limit their device and time with friends until they get and actually hold down the next job.

If getting your reluctant teen to drive and hold down a job seems like a lot of work to you, you're right it can be. However, I know that if you follow the steps outlined in this chapter, you can very likely get them to do both, and I promise you the effort will be worth it.

I'm going to end this chapter with a metaphor that captures the essence of why having high expectations of your child or teen and asking them to step out of their comfort zones and do hard things is worth your time and effort as a parent.

In Episode 158 of the No Stupid Questions podcast entitled, "Bigger Fish or Bigger Pond," Michael Maughan, one of the hosts, uses goldfish as a metaphor for life, which I'm going to paraphrase for you here.

Goldfish are among a type of species that are known as "indeterminate growers," meaning that they continue to grow throughout their lifespan. However, their ultimate size is determined by their environment.

As kids, most of us have had the experience of owning a goldfish that we likely got from a county fair or pet store. When you put a goldfish into a small aquarium, it stays more or less the same size because its growth is limited by the size of the tank. However, if you had taken that same goldfish and put it outside and into a pond, it could easily have grown to the size of a football.

The moral of the story?

We only grow as big as the spaces in which we live.

Takeaways from Chapter 15

- As is the case with having kids do chores, asking them to get their driver's license and a part-time job is part of learning how to be independent, confident, and self-reliant.
- However, relative to previous generations, fewer teenagers are getting their license and even fewer a part-time job. Researchers have speculated that this loss of independence is one of the contributors to the current teen mental health epidemic.
- Many teenagers report feeling too anxious (nervous) to drive, which is often why so many parents don't push for it. However, what we've learned about the treatment of anxiety is that avoiding anxiety-inducing situations actually makes a person's anxiety worse. In addition, some parents report not wanting their teen to drive because they feel they might be too impulsive, too inattentive, or have poor judgment.
- However, one of the great things about learning to drive is that there are multiple steps involved in getting a license and the process takes a long time. This gives nervous kids an opportunity to slowly become acclimated to driving, and for parents to push the pause button at any time for more impulsive kids to slow the process down.
- You will very likely overcome your teen's reluctance to getting their license by following the step-by-step plan outlined in this chapter.
- Similarly, many kids are reluctant to get a part-time job, but doing so is one of the best ways to help them become more mature, independent human beings.
- This same step-by-step process can also be used to effectively, and peacefully, help your reluctant teen get and keep their very first part-time job.

On Orchids and Dandelions

16

I've had the honor and privilege of working with many challenging kids over the course of my career. Kids who hurt themselves, kids who are too anxious or depressed to even leave their bedrooms, kids who run away, kids who are physically aggressive, and more, but strong-willed and oppositional kids are my favorite. In fact, they steal my heart.

I think there are two reasons why I like them so very much.

First, obviously, they are very headstrong, and while this quality can drive you as their parent up the wall, it's also a quality that I secretly admire in kids. I like that they don't just go along with things, and I think more kids would benefit from some of that nonconformity. Too much of a good quality, however, is no longer a good quality. Strong-willed and oppositional kids desperately need to acquire the ability to temper that superpower and use it in more focused, less indiscriminate ways. They get in their own way an awful lot, often behaving in ways that run counter to their own self-interests. However, if they learn the difference between when tenacity is called for and when it isn't, my goodness, that's an ability that will serve them well in future careers and in life in general.

The second reason these kids are my favorite is because they are often so very lost. Tragically so, in many cases. As I said earlier in the book, oppositional kids didn't ask to be oppositional and more difficult-to-parent, they just are. I've been convinced for years that oppositional kids come into the world this way—some sort of temperamental, biological difference that science is just beginning to understand. Imagine being born into a world where everyone is so very different from themselves. Their parents aren't like that, their brothers and sisters aren't like that, and most kids at school aren't like that. Strong-willed kids are perpetually square pegs forced into round holes. They always feel like outsiders; that there is something wrong inside them. I was in trouble sometimes

DOI: 10.4324/9781003452638-20

as a kid, and I sure didn't like that feeling, so I can't even fathom what it would be like to feel that way all of the time.

In a 2005 research study with the not-very exciting title, "Biological Sensitivity to Context: An Evolutionary-Developmental Theory of the Origins and Functions of Stress Reactivity," published in the journal *Development and Psychopathology*, researchers W. Thomas Bryce and Bruce Ellis discuss what may be genetic differences between kids who seem to thrive in just about any environment versus those who exhibit "context dependent" outcomes. To put it simply, some kids just seem to do better even in adverse situations and are naturally more resilient, while other kids are far more sensitive to their immediate environment if it's less than ideal and as a result have more behavior problems and poorer mental health.

Bryce and Ellis use two Swedish terms to illustrate the point. The first, *maskrosbarn* (dandelion child), describes children who, like the flower, seem to survive and even thrive in whatever environments they encounter. They tend to do okay no matter what. In contrast, *orkidebarn* (orchid child) are those that due to possible genetic and biological differences are much more context-sensitive. Like the orchid, these kids' survival is much more dependent on the quality of their immediate environment. Orchids, when not cared for in an ideal way, do not thrive and might even die, but when supported and nurtured, as the authors put it, an orchid is "a flower of unusual delicacy and beauty."

Anyone can grow a dandelion child. Easier-to-parent kids can be challenging at times, sure, but to raise an orchid child, well, that's something altogether different. No one will ever love your child as much as you do, and no one is better equipped to provide them with the care, affection, and support they need to blossom into the person they are meant to be.

Remember, your child or teen has absolutely no idea why they do whatever it is that drew you to this book in the first place. They don't like acting the way they do, and they're just waiting for you to gently but firmly set limits and show them how to be a better version of themselves, now and forever. Once you're able to do that, it will free up so much space in your relationship that it will allow you countless opportunities to be the gentle, loving parent that in your heart I know you long to be.

I hope this book has helped you raise your flower of unusual delicacy and beauty.

Index

Printed in the United States
by Baker & Taylor Publisher Services